Editor
Kim Fields

Editorial Project Manager
Mara Ellen Guckian

Editor-in-Chief
Sharon Coan, M.S. Ed.

Illustrator
Kelly McMahon

Cover Artist
Denise Bauer

Art Manager
Kevin Barnes

Art Director
CJae Froshay

Imaging
Ralph Olmedo, Jr.
Rosa C. See

Product Manager
Phil Garcia

Publishers
Rachelle Cracchiolo, M.S. Ed.
Mary Dupuy Smith, M.S. Ed.

Building Literacy Skills
Through Art

Pre K – 1

Author

Jennifer Dorval

Teacher Created Materials, Inc.
6421 Industry Way
Westminster, CA 92683
www.teachercreated.com.
ISBN-0-7439-3377-X
©2004 Teacher Created Materials, Inc.
Made in U.S.A.

Table of Contents

Introduction

Welcome to *Building Literacy Skills Through Art*—an exciting approach to developing literacy skills for young learners. "Literacy" refers to the ability to construct meaning through reading and writing. It is a key element in a child's academic and social success. For this reason, we should do everything possible to build literacy skills within our students. Given current academic standards, this process needs to start at a very early age.

The use of arts and crafts helps children build literacy skills in a fun, hands-on, relaxed environment. We know that children learn in different ways and within different time frames. Therefore, each class of students requires a variety of teaching methods and styles to learn necessary skills.

Each activity is presented in the following way:

✻ Objective

Each project addresses a specific literacy objective. The objective can be accomplished in one of two ways: when students do the suggested art project, or, by using the art project as part of a larger context.

✻ Links to Literacy

This section gives suggestions on how to achieve the objective stated and how to build literacy skills through the art project. The suggestions will either build skills through the process of making the art project or by using the completed project in an activity, game, story, rhyme, or pattern of language. Determine what students are capable of doing by themselves, and at what stage they will need assistance. Extension activities are suggested to meet the needs of varying skill and age levels.

✻ Materials

This section clearly outlines what is needed to complete each art activity. It includes extra items mentioned in the Links to Literacy portion of the page. The materials listed are required for making one item. Therefore, you will need the correct number of materials for each individual in your class to complete the project. The majority of the items are easily found around the house or at school. Dimensions and illustrations are provided for most of the items in the Materials Glossary (pages 204–206). Generally, the finished project is illustrated next to the materials.

✻ Art Project Instructions

This section offers you step-by-step directions to easily complete the craft to be used in the Links to Literacy section. These steps are illustrated, when necessary, to clarify what needs to be done. Read each craft page with the person or group involved in creating the craft. It is critical for children to witness adults modeling the importance of reading.

- Read the directions carefully and completely before starting a project. Make note of tools (scissors, glue guns, etc.) that are required.

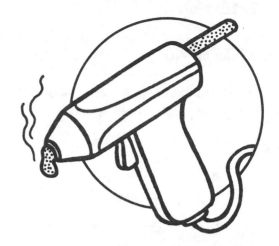

- Actively assist with crafts that require any adult supervision for safety. Projects that use a hot glue gun, stove, tools, sharp utensils, or scissors require constant adult supervision and additional help. Make certain that cords and wires are clearly visible.

- Make sure to thoroughly clean all previously used containers. Add a little bleach to the cleaning water to kill leftover bacteria.

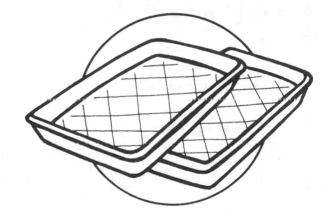

- Never use meat trays that have held raw chicken. The butcher, if asked, may be willing to donate unused meat trays.

- Cover work surfaces with a protective layer of newspaper, cardboard, plastic, or cloth.

- Model "safety first" behavior as you work with, or in front of, children. After using an implement, put it away, turn it off, or secure it to prevent injury.

- Teach children to clean up and put things in their proper places after completing a project.

- Review proper cutting procedures and the correct way to carry scissors.

ABC Apple Tree

Links to Literacy

Students can practice naming letters and sounds, sequencing alphabetically, and making words with the apples after making the ABC Apple Tree. Affix each apple on the tree using removable adhesive. Alone, or with a partner, a student pulls off each apple one at a time and says the letter name. To extend the activity, the student can say the sound that each letter makes, take off the apples in alphabetical order, or remove the apples to make words.

Materials

- 2 sheets of red construction paper
- tall potato chip container
- sheet of green Bristol paper or tagboard
- apple alphabet patterns (pages 7–8)
- brown acrylic paint or construction paper
- paintbrush
- scissors
- removable sticky adhesive or Velcro

Art Project Instructions

1. To make the tree trunk, paint the potato chip tube brown (or cover it with brown paper). Allow time to dry.

2. Cut four equal slits at the top of the tube, approximately 2" in length all around the tube.

3. Fold the Bristol paper in half; then fold it in half a second time. Produce four leafy treetops by cutting out a cloud-like shape from the twice-folded green paper.

4. Insert the treetops into the slits in the tube by carefully bending each treetop to fit into the two closest slits in the container. Put the next treetop beside the first by using one of the same slits as the previous treetop and then the next closest empty slit. Continue with the last two treetops until all four slits are filled with two pieces and the treetop is formed.

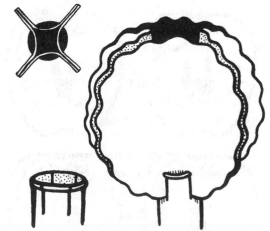

5. Reproduce the apple alphabet patterns onto red construction paper. Cut out the apples.

   (*Alternatives:* Enlarge the apple patterns or make them smaller depending on the treetop and tube sizes. Or, use 26 apple stickers printed with the letters of the alphabet instead of the patterns. To make smaller trees, use toilet paper tubes, green construction paper, and smaller red apples.)

#3377 Building Literacy Skills Through Art

Apple Alphabet Patterns (cont.)

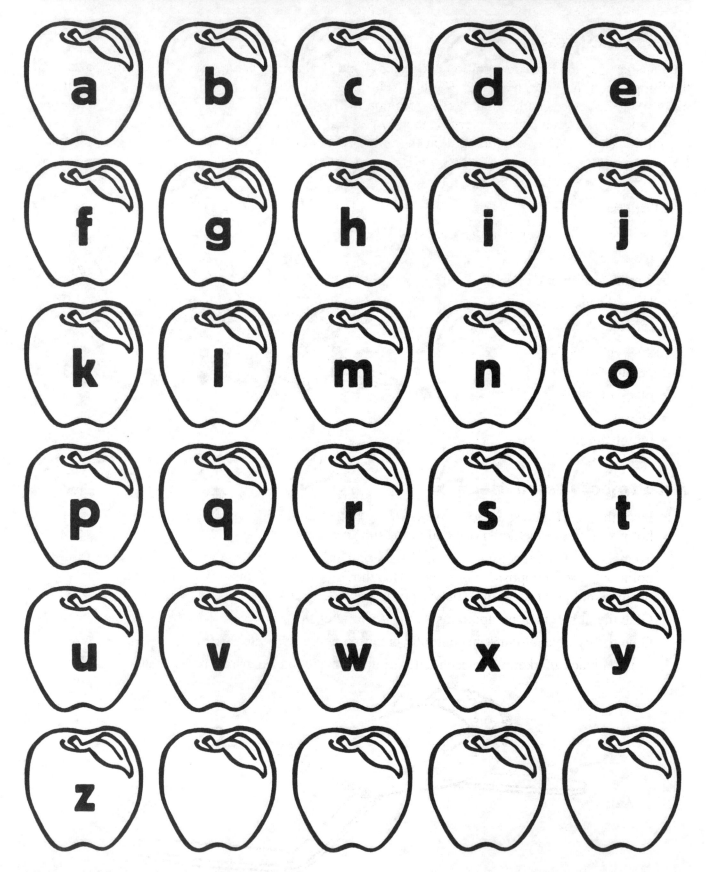

Links to Literacy

Students can review letter recognition and letter sound skills after making the frog and lily pads. Place the lily pads on the floor in a path. The lily pads can be set out in alphabetical order, or randomly, to make the game more challenging. Set the frog on the first lily pad and say the name of the letter on it. When a letter has been named correctly, the lily pad can be removed from the path and set aside. To extend the activity, write a sight word on each lily pad or have students say the letter sounds instead of the names.

Materials

- 26 large white paper plates (lilypads)
- 6 mini craft sticks
- 2 mini black pompoms
- large green pompom
- toilet paper tube
- green acrylic paint
- paintbrush
- black marker
- tape
- hot glue gun

Art Project Instructions

1. Paint the paper plates, the toilet paper tube, and the craft sticks green. Allow time to dry. Use the hot glue gun to glue down one end of the tube (as shown.)

2. To make the frog, tape four craft sticks, two on each end, to the toilet paper tube so that the sticks point outward in opposite directions. Then hot glue the remaining two craft sticks to the sticks on one end and point them in. This will form the frog's back legs.

3. Glue the large green pompom inside the opening of the toilet paper tube between the front legs.

4. Glue the two black pompoms onto the green pompom to create the frog's eyes.

5. Using a black marker, write each letter of the alphabet on a separate paper plate.

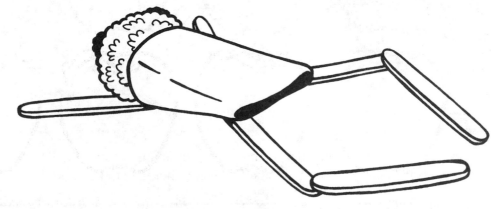

Carton Caterpillar

Objective: Letter recognition

Links to Literacy

Students can review the uppercase and lowercase versions of each letter of the alphabet after making the Carton Caterpillar. Have students write the corresponding uppercase letter on the opposite side of each egg carton cup. To extend the activity, use old magazines or flyers and cut out small pictures of things that start with each letter of the alphabet. Have students glue the cutout to the appropriate cup. To develop counting and mathematical skills, have them count each egg carton cup and the feet needed to make the caterpillar.

Materials

- 3 empty Styrofoam egg cartons
- 25 chenille stick pieces
- 2 wiggle eyes
- permanent marker
- scissors
- glue
- old magazines

Art Project Instructions

1. Cut out 26 egg carton cups and use pieces of chenille stick to join each cup to the next by pushing the chenille stick into the bottom of the cup and bending it up inside so that it stays in place.

2. Glue the wiggle eyes onto the first egg carton cup, in the front. Complete the face by drawing a nose and mouth.

3. Write a lowercase letter of the alphabet on one side of each egg carton cup.

Variation: Cut out 52 feet for the caterpillar, using the top of an egg carton and attach one foot to each side of each cup on the caterpillar with a small piece of chenille stick.

Objective: Letter recognition

Links to Literacy

Students can practice letter recognition and letter sound skills after making the Simple Sounds Snake. Alone or in small groups, have students say the names or sounds of the letters on one section of the snake's body. When all of the letters have been said, twist the section so that all of the letters now face the bottom. The object of the game is to end up with an entirely plain snake. To extend the activity, have the combination of letters on each section spell words, or use letter blends or digraphs such as /br/, /th/, /sh/, or vowels and consonants.

Materials

- pre-formed coin wrappers (cylinders)
- green paint
- paintbrush
- green construction paper
- pencil
- permanent marker
- scissors
- glue
- tape
- string
- cardboard

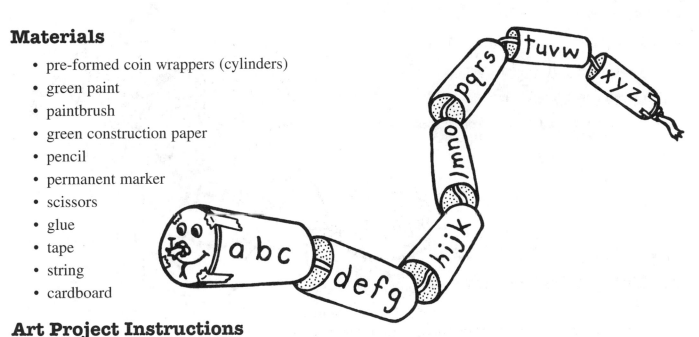

Art Project Instructions

1. Glue the end of each coin wrapper tube down. Paint the tubes green (or cover them with green paper) and allow time to dry.

2. Cut out two small circles from the green construction paper and make a snake face on one. Use the other circle to seal/close the last snake body section. Reinforce the circles by gluing them to cardboard circles.

3. Thread the string through the inside of the painted tubes to form the snake's body. The tubes will twist and rotate easily.

4. To keep the string in place, use a pencil to poke a small hole in the middle of the face and end section circle. Thread one end of the string through the hole in the face and knot it. Tape the face securely to the tube. Thread the other end of the string through the hole in the back circle. Knot the string to create the back end of the snake and tape the back to the tube.

5. Write a combination of three or four alphabet letters on each tube. The tubes form sections of the snake's body that can be turned and twisted.

Variation: Make one large class snake by using a wrapping paper tube, cut into five sections. Place students in groups, and have each group decorate a section of the snake.

Monkey Basket

Links to Literacy

Students can practice naming letters and pairing each lowercase letter of the alphabet with the corresponding uppercase letter after making the Monkey Basket and bananas. Students pull a banana out of the basket and name the letter on it. Then, they will pull out other bananas until they find the matching uppercase or lowercase letter. They should continue until all 26 pairs have been found. To enhance the activity, color code the bananas.

Materials

- 2 sheets of brown construction paper
- 4 sheets of yellow construction paper
- brown paper lunch bag
- monkey and banana patterns (pages 13–14)
- crayons or markers
- scissors
- glue

Art Project Instructions

1. Cut the top half off the paper bag.

2. Reproduce the monkey pattern onto two sheets of brown construction paper and cut them out. Cut out the gray section to create the handles.

3. Glue the monkeys to the front and back of the bag.

4. At the top, glue the monkey's hands together to form a basket.

5. Reproduce the banana patterns onto four sheets of yellow construction paper and cut out the bananas. On half of the 52 bananas, write the uppercase letters of the alphabet from A–Z. On the remaining bananas, write the lowercase letters of the alphabet from a–z.

6. Place the bananas in the Monkey Basket.

12

Banana Patterns

Links to Literacy

Students can practice letter recognition, sequencing, and beginning sound skills after making the bowl and pretend alphabet soup. Have students locate each letter of the alphabet in order, and add it to the bowl. Each time a letter is added, have students say its name and pretend that it is a wonderful ingredient being mixed in the soup. With each letter added, students can think of a food that could be used in the soup that begins with that letter.

Materials

- 26 pieces of uncooked, tube-shaped pasta
- modeling clay
- brightly colored acrylic paint
- paintbrush
- permanent marker
- rolling pin

Art Project Instructions

1. Paint the pasta many different bright colors. Allow time to dry.

2. Use the clay to make a big soup bowl. Roll the clay into a ball; then flatten and roll it out with a rolling pin. Put your palm into the center. With your other hand, shape the sides to come up around your hand. Use your fingers to continue to shape and press the clay, until you have created a big bowl.

3. Print a different letter (from A–Z) on each of the painted noodles.

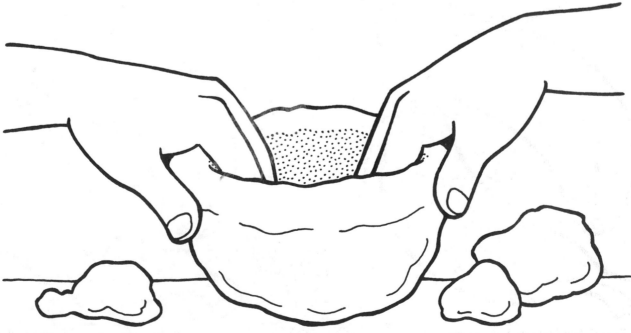

Alphabet Egg

Links to Literacy

Students can work on letter recognition skills by finding each letter of the alphabet in a box of uncooked alphabet pasta noodles before making the Alphabet Egg. Have students lay the noodles out in order to ensure they have all of the letters from A–Z. To extend the activity, have each student find the letters in his or her name using the leftover alphabet noodles. After the Alphabet Egg is complete, have the students say the alphabet and find each letter on the egg.

Materials

- 2 Styrofoam egg cups
- uncooked alphabet pasta noodles
- brightly colored acrylic paint
- paintbrush
- bowl
- paper towel or plain newsprint
- tape
- glue
- water

Art Project Instructions

1. Join the two Styrofoam egg cups to form a complete egg shape; then tape the middle together.

2. Tear small strips from paper towels or newsprint.

3. Make a mixture of two parts glue and one part water in a bowl.

4. Place a strip of paper towel over the Styrofoam egg and use a paintbrush to cover it with the glue mixture.

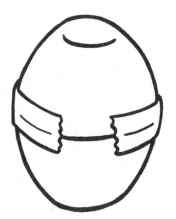

5. Completely cover the egg with the strips of paper towel and glue mixture. Allow time to dry completely.

6. Paint the Styrofoam egg and allow time to dry.

7. Glue one of each alphabet pasta letters (from A–Z) onto the egg. Allow time to dry.

Variation: Instead of painting the Styrofoam egg, paint the alphabet noodles using a variety of different colors.

16

Objective: Letter recognition

Links to Literacy

Students can practice beginning and ending sound skills after making the Pocket Panda. Choose a letter of the alphabet and label the panda's pocket with that letter. Have students cut out pictures from old magazines that begin with that letter sound. Place the pictures inside the pocket. To extend the activity, have students identify words that end with that letter sound.

Materials

- 3 large white paper plates
- panda patterns (page 18)
- black paint or crayons
- paintbrush
- pencil
- scissors
- glue
- tape or stapler
- old magazines

Art Project Instructions

1. Outline two plate rims in black, so that the majority of the plate remains white. Allow time to dry.

2. Glue one of the black rimmed plates to the top of the other plate, to form the head and body.

3. Reproduce and cut out the panda patterns. Using a pencil, trace the patterns onto the remaining plate: two ears (black), two arms (black), two legs (black), and a pocket shape (white). (**Hint:** Place the pocket shape in the center of the plate and the ears, arms, and legs around the rim of the plate.) Color or paint the pieces as indicated.

4. Glue the ears to the top of the head.

5. Glue the legs to the bottom of the body and attach one arm to each side with glue.

6. To attach the pocket, tape or staple along its edge without using any tape at the top. Press the edges onto the middle of the body. This will create the panda's stomach.

7. Draw or paint a face on the panda's head.

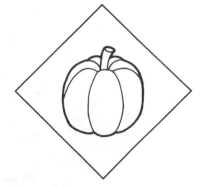

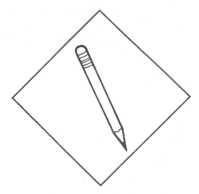

Panda Patterns

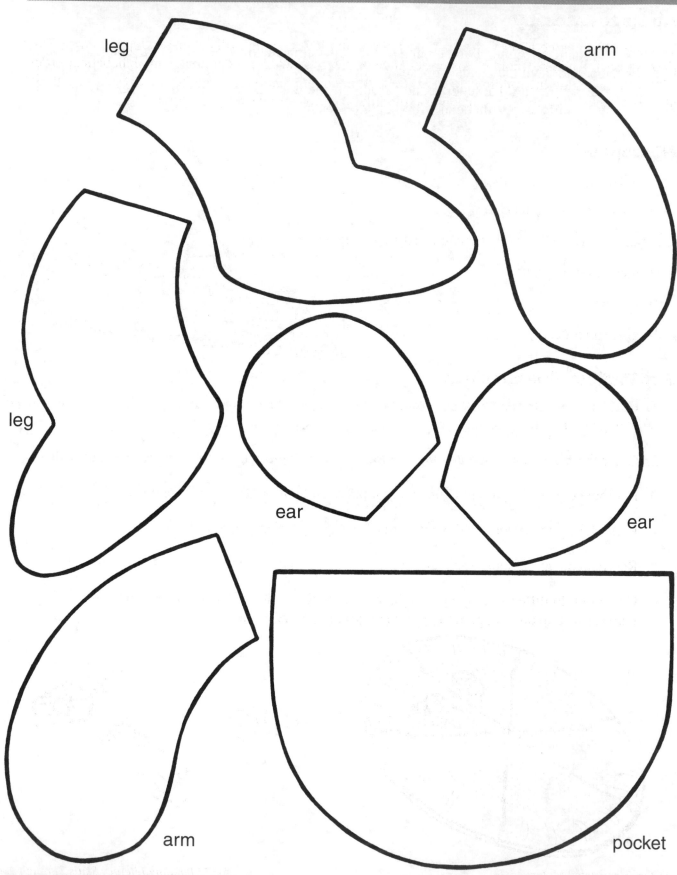

leg

arm

leg

ear

ear

arm

pocket

Links to Literacy

Students can practice letter sequencing and beginning letter sound skills after making the Paper Plate Pizzas. Each student decorates his or her slice of pizza by adding the toppings in alphabetical order. (Students may glue the toppings to the slice.) To extend the activity, have the student go through the alphabet backwards or say the name of a food that begins with each letter sound.

Materials

- 1 large white paper plate

- 26 topping patterns (pages 20–22)

- sheet of red, yellow, and green construction paper

- markers or crayons

- scissors

- glue (optional)

Art Project Instructions

1. Cut out a large triangular shape from the white paper plate. For a center activity, use a large paper plate and draw triangle slices on it.

2. Color the triangular shape a golden yellow; then mix in some red to create a basic pizza slice.

3. Reproduce page 20 onto red construction paper and cut out the pizza toppings.

4. Reproduce page 21 onto yellow paper and cut out the pizza toppings.

5. Reproduce page 22 onto green paper and cut out the pizza toppings.

6. Count out 26 different toppings and label each with a letter of the alphabet (from A–Z) using markers or crayons. If desired, glue the toppings to the pizza slice.

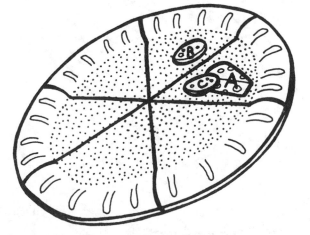

Pizza Topping Patterns

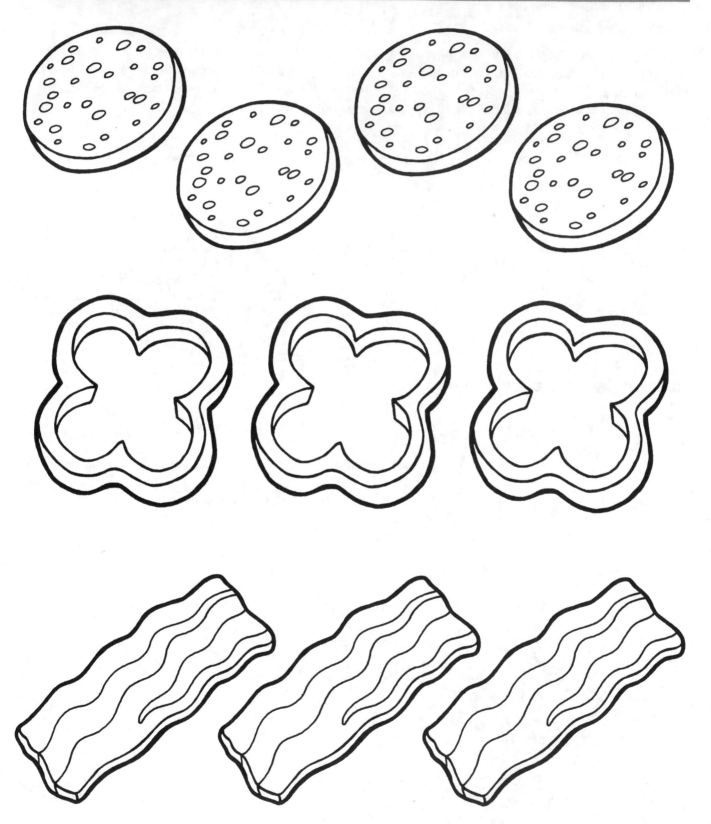

20

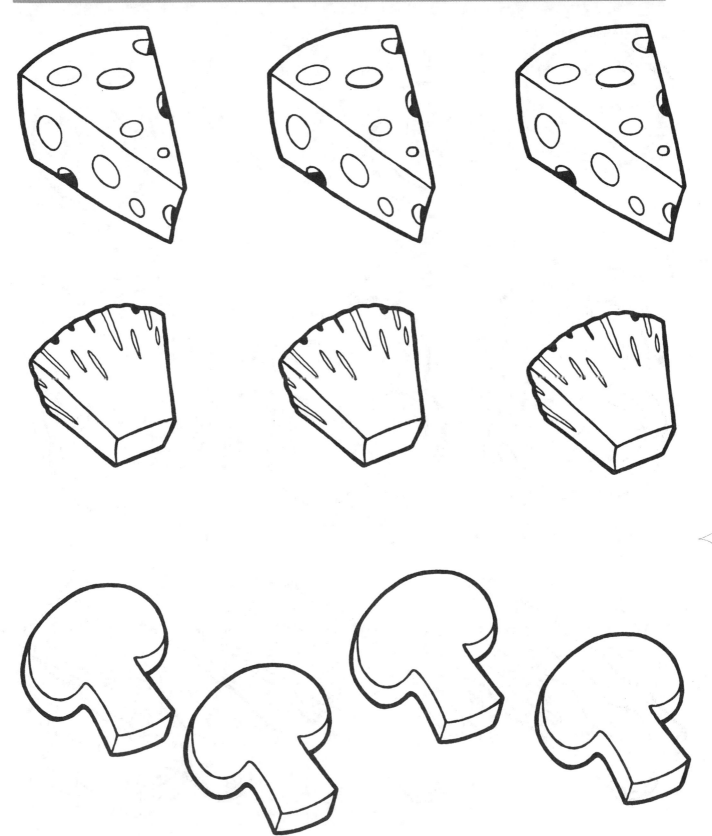

Pizza Topping Patterns (Cont.)

22

Links to Literacy

Students can polish their letter recognition skills after making the A-Bee-C Hive. Place the beehive on a flat surface. Use a thick black felt pen or alphabet stickers to label each of the honeycombs that create the hive with a different letter of the alphabet (from A–Z). Have each student take a turn at dropping his or her bee onto the hive and naming the letter that the bee landed on. The student may lift up the bee to look at the letter and name it. To extend the activity, the student may look around the bee to see which letters are to each side of the bee and then name the letter the bee landed on.

Materials: Class Beehive

- twenty-six 4" (10 cm) wide strips of thin cardboard
- yellow acrylic paint and paintbrushes
- alphabet stickers or a thick black felt pen
- glue
- rubber bands

Art Project Instructions

1. Paint the strips of cardboard yellow and allow time to dry.

2. With each strip of cardboard, put glue on one side and then tightly roll the strip like a jellyroll. Press together and hold or use a rubber band to keep it in place until it dries. Repeat for all.

3. To make the beehive, use the 26 rolls and glue them together to form a triangular hive shape, by starting with 2 rolls at the top, then 3, then 4, 5, 6, and another row of 6.

Materials: Bee

- 3 black chenille sticks
- paper lunch bag
- bee patterns (page 24)
- yellow and black acrylic paint
- paintbrush

- pencil
- crayons or markers
- scissors
- rubber bands
- old newspapers

Art Project Instructions

1. Paint the paper bag in black and yellow horizontal stripes. Allow time to dry. Scrunch up old newspaper and stuff the painted bag until it is full. Use a rubber band to close off the top so that it stays together.

2. Poke three holes in each side of the bag with a sharpened pencil to create spaces for the bee's legs. Cut two chenille sticks into thirds and put them in the holes to create six bee legs.

3. Cut the remaining chenille stick in half to create antennae and attach each in one of the circles on the head as marked. Shape the chenille sticks to look like antennae.

4. Reproduce, color, and cut out the bee patterns. Glue the head to the end of the bag. Glue the wings to the bag as shown, by folding the tabs under.

Bee Patterns

Tab

Tab

24

Links To Literacy

Students can review letter recognition and matching skills after making the Bath Full of Bubbles. Place the bubbles faceup in the bathtub container. Students pick up a bubble letter and find the corresponding uppercase or lowercase letter. The students can take turns with a partner or play individually. To extend the activity, students can flip the bubbles over and play a concentration game with the letters.

Materials

- 2 sheets of blue cardstock
- baby wipes container or shoebox
- bubble patterns (pages 26–27)
- clear cellophane or plastic wrap
- scissors
- tape
- thick, gray chenille stick

Art Project Instructions

1. To make the bathtub, peel any stickers off the baby wipes container and remove the lid.

2. To make a faucet, bend the chenille stick to give it a hook and tape it inside the container.

3. To make pretend water, scrunch up cellophane or plastic wrap and place it in the container.

4. Reproduce the bubble patterns onto cardstock. Cut out the bubbles. You will need 26 lowercase bubbles and 26 uppercase bubbles.

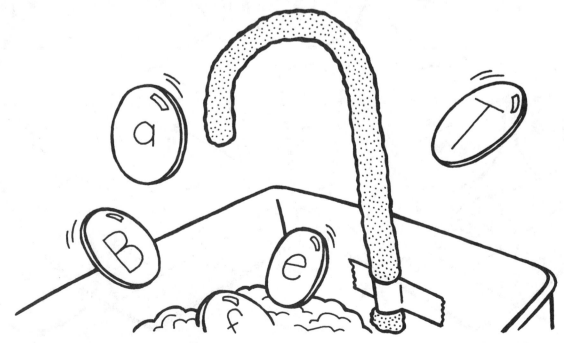

Bubble Patterns

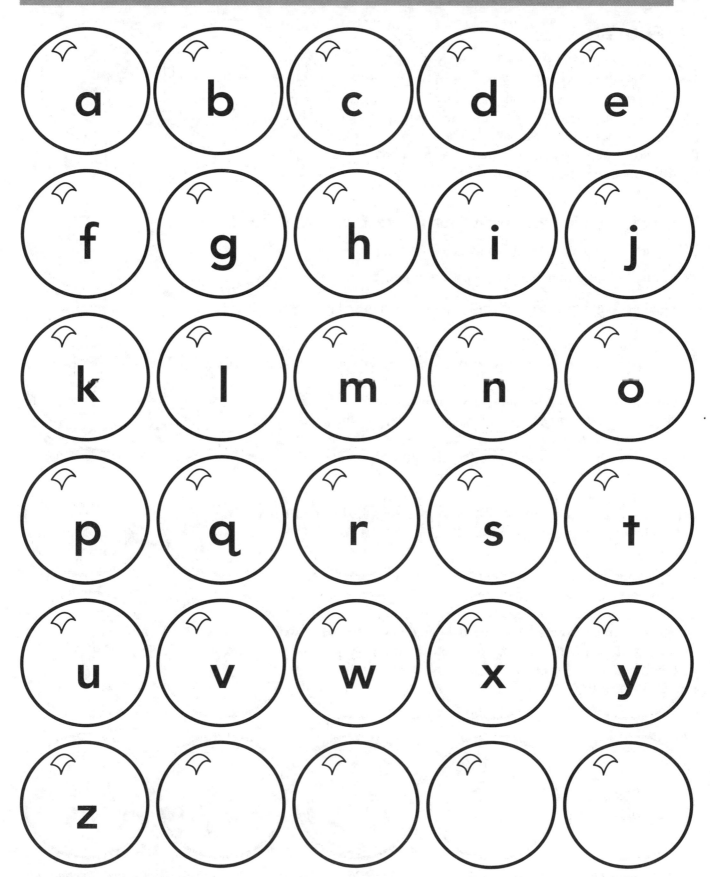

#3377 Building Literacy Skills Through Art

Alphabet Classification Containers

Objective: Classifying skills

Links to Literacy

This project is designed to replace the plain milk-carton containers, labeled from A–Z, found in many classrooms. The idea is to help students recognize letter-sound relationships by classifying different pictures or small objects and placing them in the correct containers. For example, a picture of an ant or a small apple would be placed in the **Aa** container, a picture of a bat or a small bouncy ball would go in the **Bb** container, and so on.

Materials: For all Alphabet Classification Containers

- picture cutouts from old magazines
- small objects that begin with different letters

The plain containers are excellent for putting items and pictures in, but students usually are not involved in making the containers. The projects listed for the Alphabet Classification Containers should not be done solely by the teacher or an adult helper, but rather by the students. This can be accomplished in many different ways. If you would like just one set of containers for the classroom, have students work alone or in a small group to complete the containers. With a group of 26 students, it will work perfectly for each student to make 1 letter container. If you feel the students will have difficulty, break them up into groups and assign each group 2 or 3 different letter projects to complete. To extend the activity, each person or group can be responsible for presenting the featured letter to the class and explaining the sound(s) that letter makes.

Recognizing and learning the sound(s) each new letter makes is a very important skill to be mastered. Therefore, students should create each project as they learn a letter or sound. If you choose to have each student create his or her own containers, he or she will then be equipped with a set of Alphabet Classification Containers to take home and use for practicing letter recognition and letter-sound relationship skills.

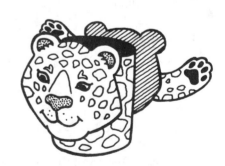

Links to Literacy

Students can practice letter recognition, letter-sound relationship, and classification skills after making the Alligator Container. Have the students fill the container with small objects and picture cutouts of things that begin with the letter **Aa**.

Materials

- tissue box or other rectangular box
- alligator patterns (pages 30–31)
- green acrylic paint or green paper
- paintbrush
- crayons or markers
- scissors
- glue
- pictures and small objects that begin with the letter **Aa**

Art Project Instructions

1. Cut a hole in the top of a rectangle box or use a pre-cut tissue box.

2. Use green acrylic paint to cover the sides of the box (or cover it with paper). Apply a second coat if it doesn't completely cover the box. Allow time to dry.

3. Reproduce, color, and cut out the alligator head and lower jaw patterns.

4. Attach the head to the front of the painted box by folding Tab A down and affixing it to the box. Apply glue to Tab B of the teeth piece and attach it underneath the box at the front.

5. Reproduce, color, and cut out the alligator legs and tail patterns.

6. Glue two legs to each side of the alligator's body.

7. Apply glue to the back of the box at the top and attach Tab C of the tail.

Alligator Patterns

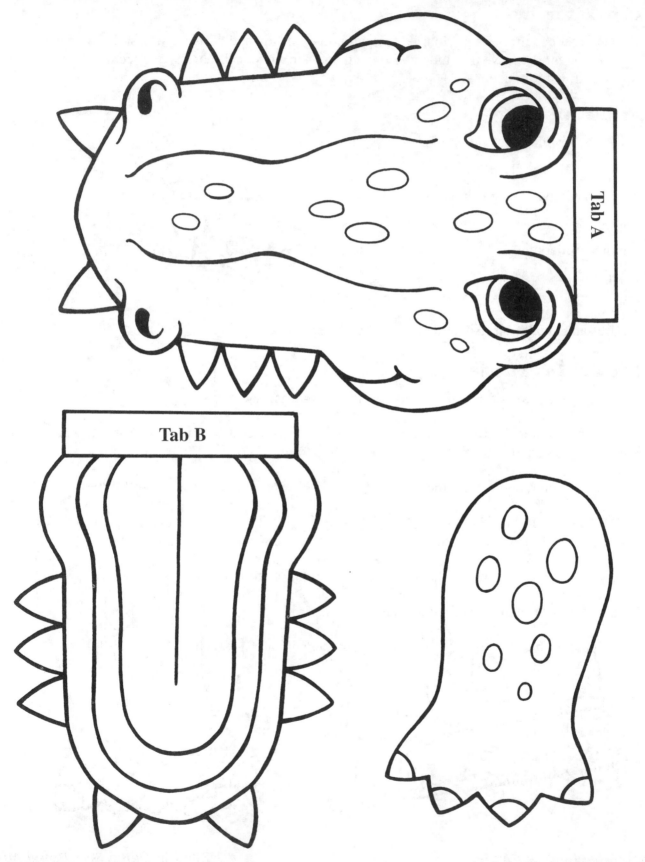

Tab A

Tab B

30

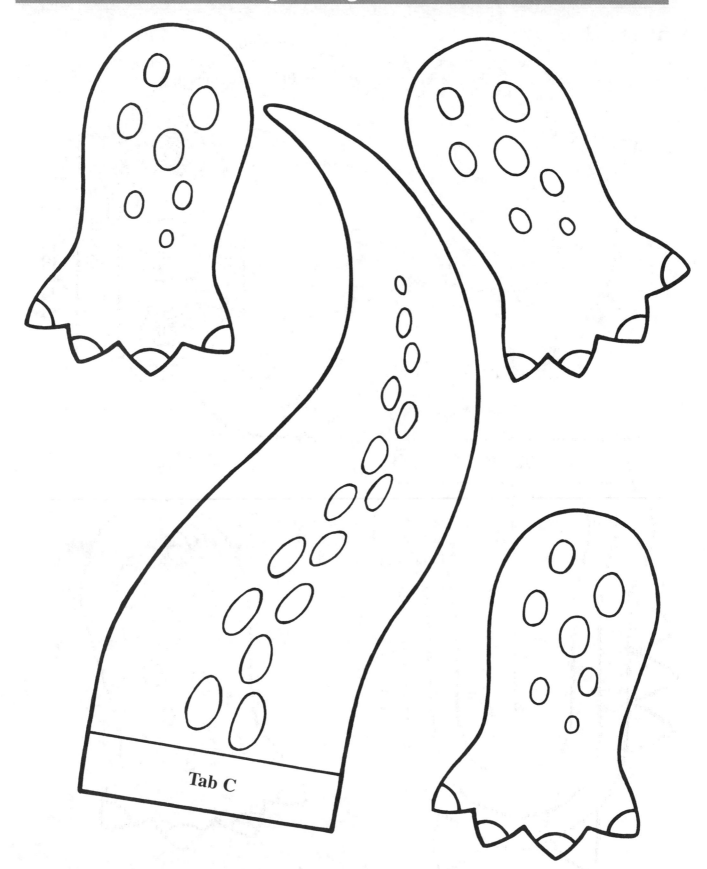

Tab C

Classification Containers

Links to Literacy

Students can practice letter recognition, letter-sound relationship, and classification skills after making the Beach Bag. Have the students fill the container with small objects and picture cutouts of things that begin with the letter **Bb**.

Materials

- paper lunch bag

- beach bag patterns (page 33)

- crayons or markers

- glue

- scissors

- pictures and small objects that begin with the letter **Bb**

Art Project Instructions

1. Reproduce twice, color, and cut out the beach bag patterns.

2. Fold the beach patterns along the dotted lines and glue them around the paper bag to cover the bottom half of the bag.

3. Cut off the excess bag around the top of the beach patterns.

4. Apply glue to the tab on each sun pattern.

5. Glue one sun to the inside top of the front and one to the back of the bag. The sun pieces create the bag handles.

   Optional: To create actual handles cut out the interior semi-circles of the suns before attaching them to the sides.

Tab

Links to Literacy

Students can practice letter recognition, letter-sound relationship, and classification skills after making the Cat Container. Have the students fill the container with small objects and picture cutouts of things that begin with the letter **Cc**.

Materials

- 2 small, Styrofoam takeout containers

- cat patterns (page 35)

- crayons or markers

- glue

- scissors

- pictures and small objects that begin with the letter **Cc**

Art Project Instructions

1. Close the lids of the two takeout containers. Glue one box to the other, with the lid openings facing in opposite directions.

2. Reproduce, color, and cut out the cat patterns.

3. To create the cat's mouth, glue the head of the cat to the top of the container that opens up.

4. Glue the body of the cat to the three remaining sections of the containers. (The bottom box will not be opened up, as it faces the back).

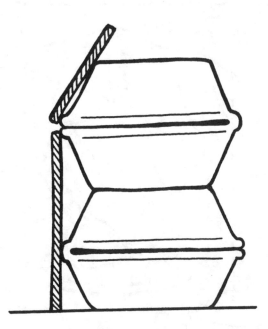

Classification Containers

Links to Literacy

Students can practice letter recognition, letter-sound relationship, and classification skills after making the Dinosaur Container. Have the students fill the container with small objects and picture cutouts of things that begin with the letter **Dd**.

Materials

- large milk carton
- dinosaur patterns (page 37–38)
- green construction paper
- crayons or markers
- glue
- scissors
- pictures and small objects that begin with the letter **Dd**
- tape

Art Project Instructions

1. Glue the opened carton back to its original unopened position.

2. Cover the milk carton by taping on green construction paper.

3. With the help of an adult, cut out a large circle or oval shape in the middle of one side of the milk carton. This will be the stomach of the dinosaur. Cut the oval on one of the sides where the top is pointed.

4. Reproduce, color, and cut out the dinosaur patterns.

5. Fold the head in half, along the dotted line. Then fold along Tabs A and B. Apply glue to Tab A and glue Tab B atop it.

6. Apply glue to the underside of the head and glue the head to the top of the carton.

7. Glue feet to the bottom sides and arms to the top sides of the milk carton.

8. Fold Tab C under. Apply glue to Tab C and glue the tail to the bottom back side of the carton.

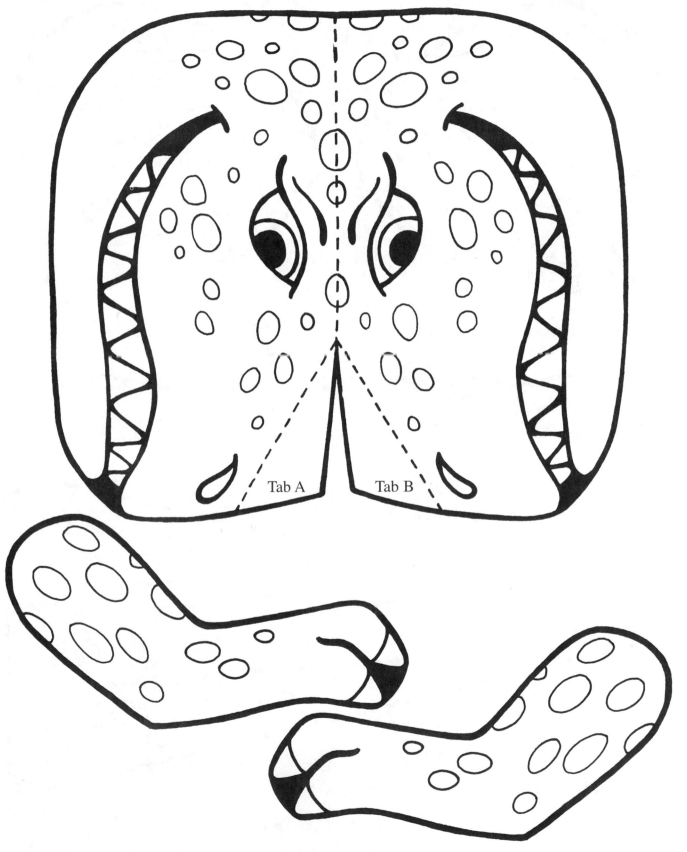

Tab A Tab B

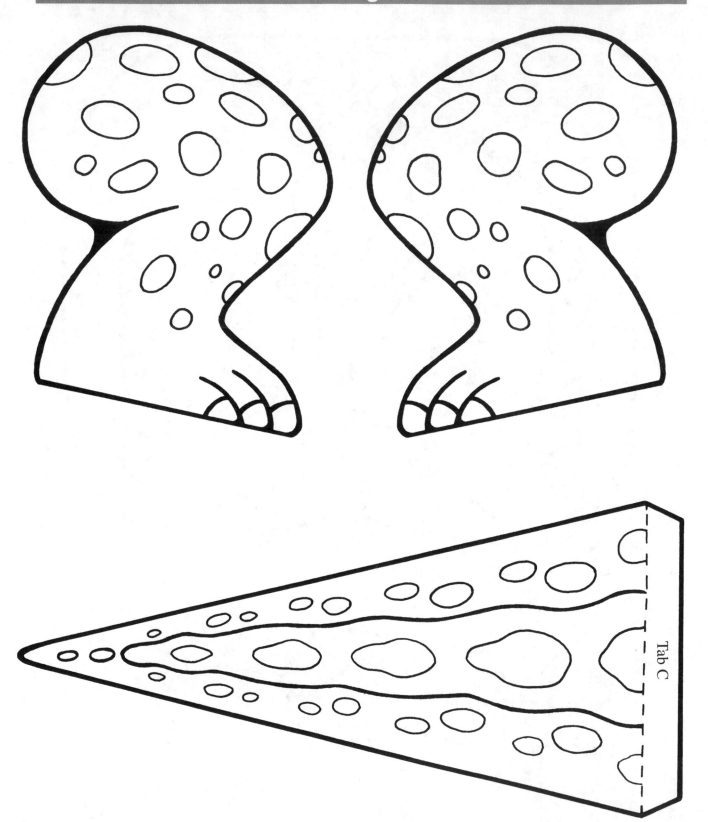

Tab C

Links to Literacy

Students can practice letter recognition, letter-sound relationship, and classification skills after making the Elephant Container. Have the students fill the container with small objects and picture cutouts of things that begin with the letter **Ee**.

Materials

- small, round nuts container

- elephant patterns (page 40)

- crayons or markers

- glue

- tape

- scissors

- gray paper or gray paint

- pictures and small objects that begin with the letter **Ee**

Art Project Instructions

1. Reproduce, color, and cut out the elephant patterns.

2. Cover the can with gray paper or paint.

3. Tape the face of the elephant to the front of the container.

4. To make the ears, fold Tabs A and B under. Apply glue to the tabs and attach the ears to the sides of the container.

5. To make the trunk, fold Tabs C and D out and glue the trunk pieces together. Cut the slit in the center of the elephant's face.

6. Push the trunk through from the back of the slit to the front.

7. Tape or glue the "folded-out" tabs to the back of the elephant's face.

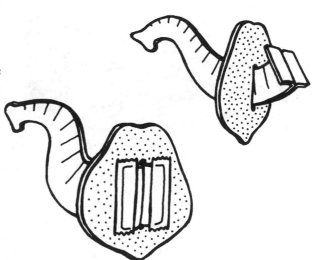

Elephant Patterns

Links to Literacy

Students can practice letter recognition, letter-sound relationship, and classification skills after making the Fish Container. Have the students fill the container with small objects and picture cutouts of things that begin with the letter **Ff**.

Materials

- egg carton lid
- fish patterns (page 42)
- crayons or markers
- scissors
- glue
- tape
- pictures and small objects that begin with the letter **Ff**

Art Project Instructions

1. Reproduce, color, and cut out the fish patterns. To create the Fish Container, fold down Tab D on the head. Glue it to one of the shorter ends of the egg carton lid so that the outside of the lid is facing down and the open side is up.

2. Glue one fin to each side of the lid by applying the glue to Tab A and folding it back.

3. Glue the tail fin to back of the lid by applying the glue to Tab B and folding it back.

4. Fold the dorsal fin (top fin) along the dotted line. Apply glue to each Tab C. Glue the fin in the center of the open lid.

Fish Patterns

Tab D

Tab A

Tab A

Tab B

Tab C

Tab C

42

Links to Literacy

Students can practice letter recognition, letter-sound relationship, and classification skills after making the Grandma Container. Have the students fill the container with small objects and picture cutouts of things that begin with the letter **Gg**.

Materials

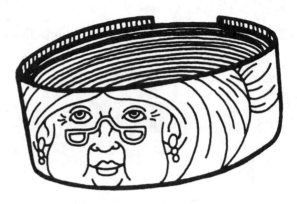

- large, round tuna or chicken can
- grandma pattern (See below.)
- glue
- scissors
- construction paper
- crayons or markers
- pictures and small objects that begin with the letter **Gg**

Art Project Instructions

1. Reproduce, color, and cut out the grandma pattern.
2. Cut a strip of construction paper to cover the side of the can.
3. Glue the strip of paper around the can.
4. Glue the pattern around the can.

Grandma Pattern

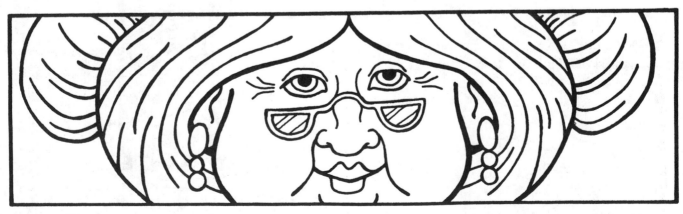

Classification Containers

Links to Literacy

Students can practice letter recognition, letter-sound relationship, and classification skills after making the Haunted House. Have the students fill the container with small objects and picture cutouts of things that begin with the letter **Hh**.

Materials

- two 2" x 9" (5 cm x 23 cm) black construction-paper strips (Strips should be the same size as the sides of the cereal box.)

- small cereal box

- haunted house patterns (pages 45–46)

- scissors

- white chalk or crayon

- crayons or markers

- glue

- pictures and small objects that begin with the letter **Hh**

Art Project Instructions

1. Cut the top off the cereal box.

2. Reproduce, color, and cut out the Haunted House patterns.

3. Glue the appropriate pattern onto the front and back of the box.

4. Decorate the black construction-paper strips with white chalk windows or ghosts.

5. Glue one strip on each side of the cereal box.

Front

45 #3377 Building Literacy Skills Through Art

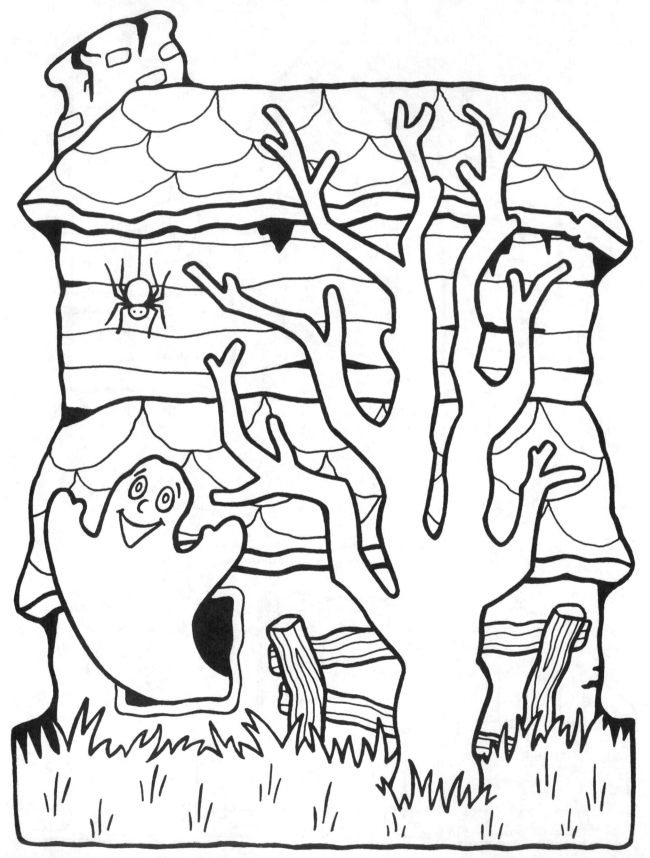

Links to Literacy

Students can practice letter recognition, letter-sound relationship, and classification skills after making the Island Container. Have the students fill the container with small objects and picture cutouts of things that begin with the letter **Ii**.

Materials

- 2 sheets of Bristol paper or tagboard
- cardboard
- small powdered drink container
- brown toilet paper tubes
- blue, brown, and green acrylic paint
- paintbrush
- green construction paper
- tape
- glue
- bowl
- water
- scissors
- newsprint or paper towel
- pictures and small objects that begin with the letter **Ii**

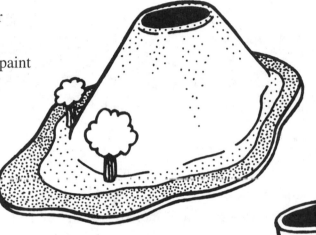

Art Project Instructions

1. Cut the cardboard in a large, uneven circular shape.

2. Place the drink container over to one side of the circular cardboard base so that it is not completely centered. Tape the container securely in place.

3. Without covering the hole in the container, place two sheets of Bristol paper around the tin, and attach it to the cardboard base with tape. Tape the Bristol paper to the top of the container. This will create a hill-like island.

4. Mix two parts glue with one part water.

5. Tear strips of newsprint and use the glue mixture and a paintbrush to paste the newsprint to the Bristol paper and cardboard. This will give the Island texture and sturdiness. Be careful not to cover the hole of the container.

6. After everything is dry, paint the Island green. Paint the bottom base blue to create the look of water around the island.

7. To create the look of trees, glue some trees made from toilet paper tubes and green construction paper, such as the ones described on page 6. Cut tubes in half for shorter trees.

Classification Containers

Links to Literacy

Students can practice letter recognition, letter-sound relationship, and classification skills after making the Jaguar Container. Have the students fill the container with small objects and picture cutouts of things that begin with the letter **Jj**.

Materials

- small powdered-drink container
- jaguar patterns (See below and page 49.)
- crayons or markers
- yellow construction paper
- glue
- scissors
- pictures and small objects that begin with the letter **Jj**

Art Project Instructions

1. Reproduce, color, and cut out the jaguar patterns.
2. Cover the can with yellow construction paper. Use markers or crayons to add spots.
3. Glue the jaguar's head to the front of the drink container and the back of his head to the back.
4. Apply glue to the marked areas on the jaguar's paws and glue them to the back of the head (as marked).
5. Add spots to the back of the paws.

Jaguar Paw Patterns

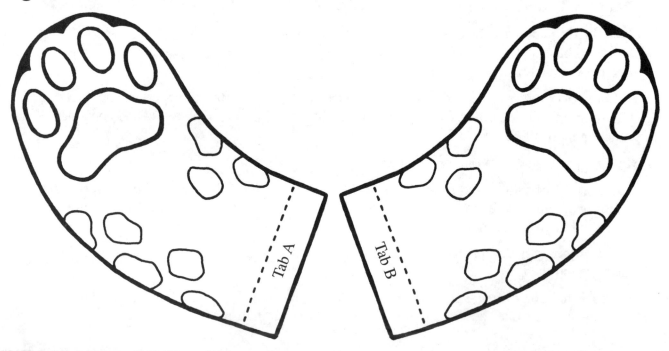

Tab A   Tab B

Tab A

Tab B

Links to Literacy

Students can practice letter recognition, letter-sound relationship, and classification skills after making the King Container. Have the students fill the container with small objects and picture cutouts of things that begin with the letter **Kk**.

Materials

- large, round tuna or chicken can

- construction paper

- king pattern (See below.)

- glue

- scissors

- crayons or markers

- pictures and small objects that begin with the letter **Kk**

Art Project Instructions

1. Reproduce, color, and cut out the king pattern.

2. Cut a strip of construction paper to cover the side of the can.

3. Glue the strip of paper around the can.

4. Glue the pattern around the can.

King Pattern

Links to Literacy

Students can practice letter recognition, letter-sound relationship, and classification skills after making the Leaf Container. Have the students fill the container with small objects and picture cutouts of things that begin with the letter **Ll**.

Materials

- cracker box

- 3 small pudding boxes

- real leaves or leaf patterns (page 52)

- tape

- white paper

- glue

- scissors

- crayons

- pictures and small objects that begin with the letter **Ll**

Art Project Instructions

1. Cut the top off the rectangular cracker box.

2. Place the three pudding boxes together and tape them as shown.

3. Form an "L" shape with the boxes by putting them against the cracker box, with the opening of the boxes facing upward. Tape the pudding boxes securely to the cracker box.

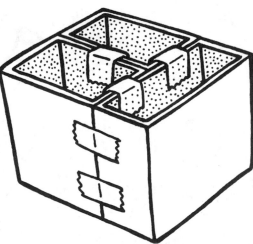

4. If the trees have leaves on them, collect some of the leaves and do leaf rubbings with a crayon on white paper. If leaves are unavailable, reproduce, color, and cut out the leaf patterns and glue them onto white paper. Cover the box with the paper.

5. Cover the Leaf Container with the decorated white paper by attaching the paper with tape or glue.

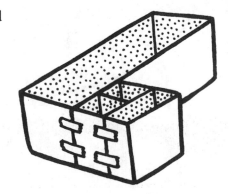

Leaf Patterns

Links to Literacy

Students can practice letter recognition, letter-sound relationship, and classification skills after making the Mini Microwave Container. Have the students fill the container with small objects and picture cutouts of things that begin with the letter **Mm**.

Materials

- shoebox with lid

- mini microwave patterns (page 54)

- white or black construction paper

- pencil

- scissors

- packing tape

- glue

- thick, black chenille stick

- pictures and small objects that begin with the letter **Mm**

- crayons or markers

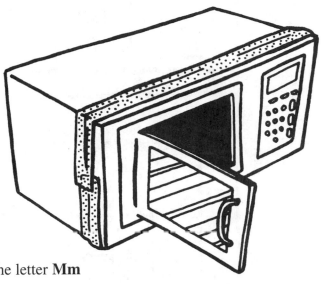

Art Project Instructions

1. Reproduce, color, and cut out the mini microwave patterns.

2. Glue the microwave door on the left and the control panel on the right of the shoebox lid.

3. With a pencil, carefully poke two small holes (where marked) in the microwave door. Insert one end of the black chenille stick into one hole and the other end of the chenille stick into the other hole. This will be the microwave door handle. When it looks like a small handle, bend the chenille stick at the back to hold it in place.

4. Cut along the dotted lines on the microwave door (through the lid), so that you can open and close it.

5. Cover the box by gluing white or black paper around all four sides.

6. Place the lid on the box, and use the packing tape to secure it in place.

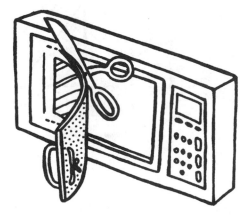

Mini Microwave Patterns

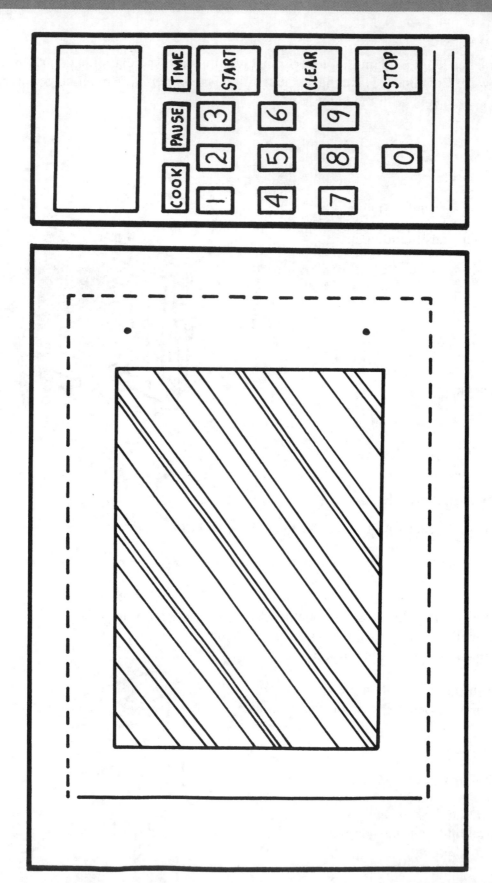

Links to Literacy

Students can practice letter recognition, letter-sound relationship, and classification skills after making the Nest Container. Have the students fill the container with small objects and picture cutouts of things that begin with the letter **Nn**.

Materials

- round, plastic individual (microwave) pasta container, large margarine tub, or whipped cream tub

- bird and egg patterns (page 56)

- sheet of yellow and brown construction paper

- cardstock

- crayons or markers

- scissors

- glue

- pictures and small objects that begin with the letter **Nn**

- Optional: chenille sticks

Art Project Instructions

1. Cut or tear strips from the yellow and brown construction paper, with more yellow than brown.

2. Randomly glue the strips of paper onto the plastic container, until the plastic is completely covered. This is to give the effect of a bird's nest.

3. Reproduce the bird and the egg patterns on cardstock or heavy paper. Color and cut out the bird and the eggs. And chenille stick legs to the bird if appropriate.

4. On the inside edge, at the back of the bowl, glue the bird so that it appears that the bird is in the nest.

5. On the inside edge, at the front of the bowl, glue the eggs in the nest.

Bird and Egg Patterns

56

Links to Literacy

Students can practice letter recognition, letter-sound relationship, and classification skills after making the Owl Container. Have the students fill the container with small objects and picture cutouts of things that begin with the letter **Oo**.

Materials

- 2 sheets of brown or gray construction paper
- large milk carton
- owl patterns (pages 58–59)
- crayons or markers
- glue
- scissors
- tape
- pictures and small objects that begin with the letter **Oo**

Art Project Instructions

1. Cut off the top of the milk carton, so that the top is wide open to form the container.

2. Using tape to hold it in place, cover the carton with construction paper. This will allow the patterns to adhere more easily.

3. Reproduce, color, and cut out the owl patterns.

4. Attach the front of the owl to the front of the milk carton container with glue.

5. Glue one wing to each side of the container.

6. Glue the owl's talons to the bottom of the body in the front.

7. Glue the back of the owl to the back of the container. Do not apply glue to the tail. Instead fold the pattern along the dotted line so the tail sticks out in back.

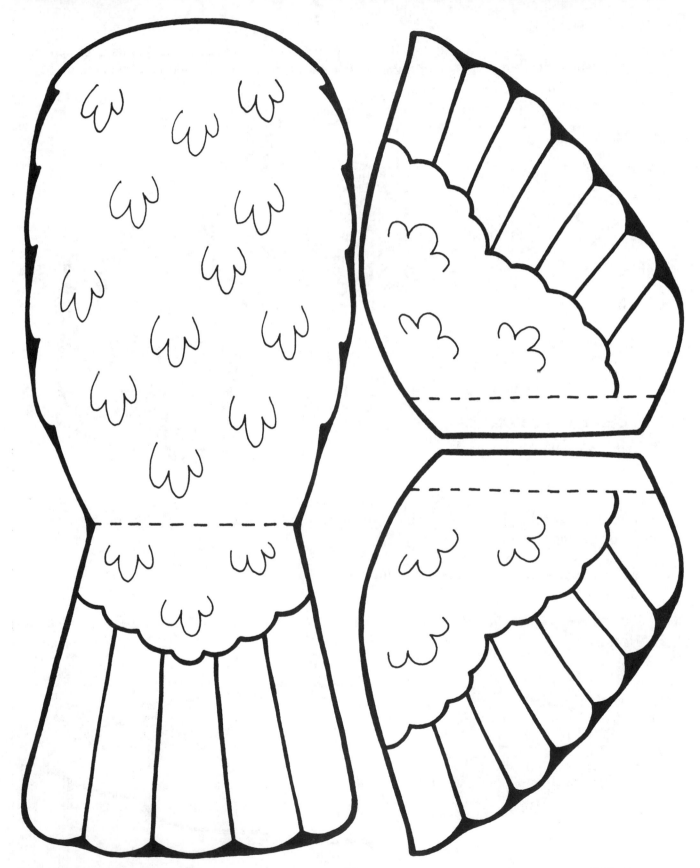

Classification Containers

Links to Literacy

Students can practice letter recognition, letter-sound relationship, and classification skills after making the Puppy Container. Have the students fill the container with small objects and picture cutouts of things that begin with the letter **Pp**.

Materials

- paper fastener

- paper lunch bag

- puppy patterns (pages 60–61)

- glue

- scissors

- crayons or markers

- pictures and small objects that begin with the letter **Pp**

Art Project Instructions

1. Cut the top half off the paper bag.

2. Reproduce, color, and cut out the puppy patterns.

3. Glue the head of the puppy to the front of the paper bag; glue the backside of the puppy to the back of the bag.

4. Carefully attach the tail of the puppy to the back end using the paper fastener, so that the tail can wag from side to side.

Tail Pattern

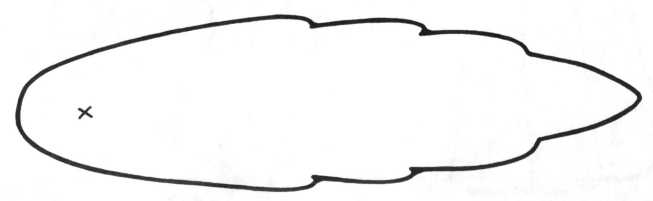

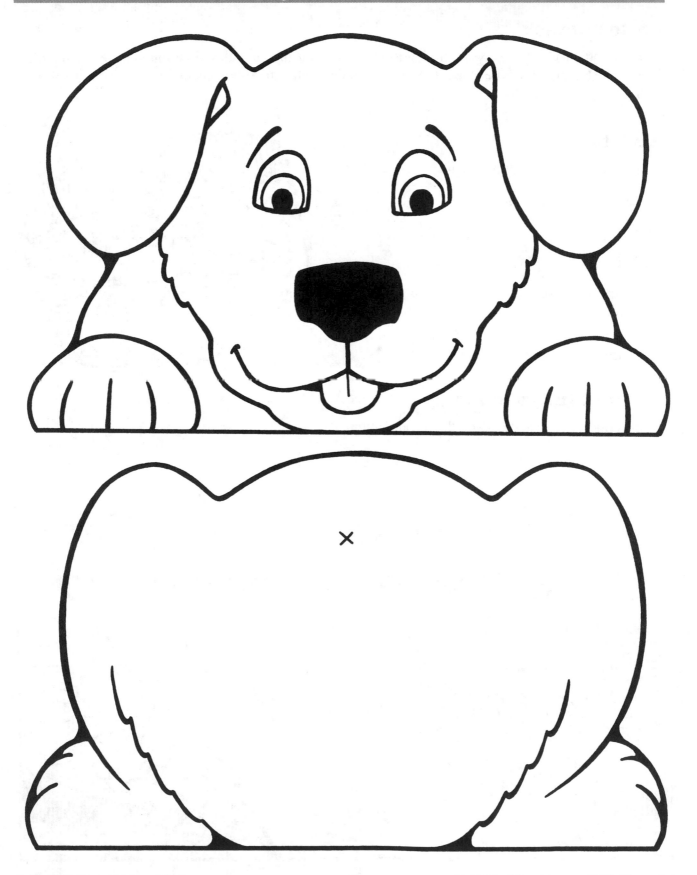

Classification Containers

Links to Literacy

Students can practice letter recognition, letter-sound relationship, and classification skills after making the Queen Container. Have the students fill the container with small objects and picture cutouts of things that begin with the letter **Qq**.

Materials

- large, round tuna or chicken can
- queen pattern (See below.)
- glue
- scissors
- crayons or markers
- pictures and small objects that begin with the letter **Qq**
- construction paper

Art Project Instructions

1. Reproduce, color, and cut out the queen pattern.

2. Cut a strip of construction paper to cover the side of the can.

3. Glue the strip of paper around the can.

4. Glue the pattern to fit around the can.

Links to Literacy

Students can practice letter recognition, letter-sound relationship, and classification skills after making the Raccoon Container. Have the students fill the container with small objects and picture cutouts of things that begin with the letter **Rr**.

Materials

- 2 sheets of brown or gray construction paper

- tissue box

- raccoon patterns (page 64)

- glue

- scissors

- crayons or markers

- pictures and small objects that begin with the letter **Rr**

Art Project Instructions

1. Cover the box in brown or gray paper on the longer sides.

2. Reproduce, color, and cut out the raccoon patterns.

3. Color the mask black and make black stripes on the tail.

4. Fold Tab A under and glue the head of the raccoon to one end of the box. This will be the front.

5. Glue the tail (Tab B) to the other end of the box, so that it is sticking up.

6. Glue two feet (Tab C) to each side of the body of the raccoon.

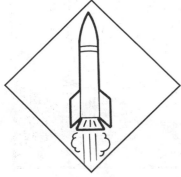
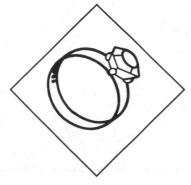
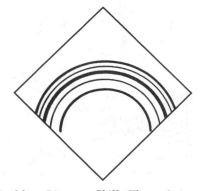

Raccoon Patterns

Raccoon Head, Tail, and Feet

Tab C

Tab C

Tab C

Tab C

Tab A

Tab B

64

Links to Literacy

Students can practice letter recognition, letter-sound relationship, and classification skills after making the Santa Container. Have the students fill the container with small objects and picture cutouts of things that begin with the letter **Ss**.

Materials

- oatmeal container or small coffee can

- Santa patterns (page 66)

- red acrylic paint and a paintbrush or red paper

- strip of black construction paper

- cotton balls

- glue

- crayons or markers

- scissors

- pictures and small objects that begin with the letter **Ss**

Art Project Instructions

1. Paint the container red and allow time to dry. (Covering the can in red paper will also work.)

2. Reproduce, color, and cut out the Santa patterns.

3. Glue the head to the top half of the container.

4. To make a belt, cut a long strip of black construction paper, and glue it around the container below Santa's head.

5. Glue the buckle over the belt in the front of the container.

6. To create the fur trim of Santa's coat, glue cotton balls all around the container just below the belt.

7. Glue the boots to the bottom front of the container underneath the trim.

8. To make the arms, fold Tabs A and B under. Apply glue and attach the arms to the sides of the container.

Links to Literacy

Students can practice letter recognition, letter-sound relationship, and classification skills after making the Tooth Container. Have the students fill the container with small objects and picture cutouts of things that begin with the letter **Tt**.

Materials

- 4 Styrofoam egg cups
- small Styrofoam takeout container
- scissors
- tape
- pictures and small objects that begin with the letter **Tt**

Art Project Instructions

1. Cut or tear the lid off the takeout container, as you only need half to make the Tooth Container.
2. Turn the container over, so that the open end is facing down.
3. On top of the container, place an egg cup in each corner, with the open end facing down.
4. Tape each egg cup in place.
5. Turn the container over to reveal your Tooth Container.

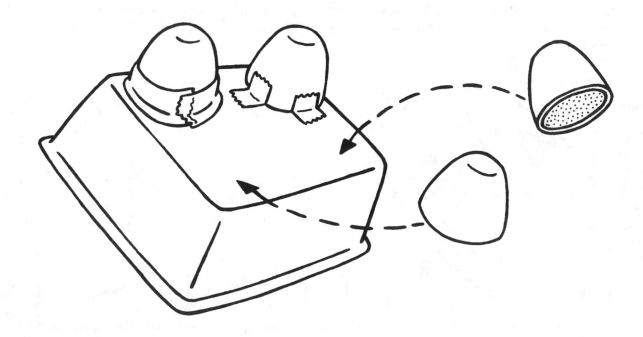

Links to Literacy

Students can practice letter recognition, letter-sound relationship, and classification skills after making the Upside-Down Umbrella Container. Have the students fill the container with small objects and picture cutouts of things that begin with the letter **Uu**.

Materials

- white paper bowl

- bright colored paints

- paintbrush

- thick chenille stick

- pencil

- tape

- pictures and small objects that begin with the letter **Uu**

Art Project Instructions

1. Paint the inside and outside of the paper bowl using bright colors, and allow time to dry.

2. Using a pencil, carefully poke a small hole in the center of the bowl.

3. Insert a chenille stick into the hole and secure it in place by bending it underneath the bowl and taping it down. At the other end of the chenille stick, form a hook shape. This will be the umbrella handle.

Vv Is for Violets Vase

Links to Literacy

Students can practice letter recognition, letter-sound relationship, and classification skills after making the Violet Vase. Have the students fill the container with small objects and picture cutouts of things that begin with the letter **Vv**.

Materials

- plastic or glass peanut butter jar
- light purple tissue paper
- violet patterns (page 70)
- glue
- scissors
- crayons or markers
- pictures and small objects that begin with the letter **Vv**
- green chenille sticks (optional)

Art Project Instructions

1. Reproduce, color, and cut out the violet patterns.

2. Tear the light purple tissue paper into small pieces.

3. Cover the outside of the jar with glue. Do not put glue at the bottom of the jar.

4. Apply the tissue pieces to the glue and let the vase dry.

5. Glue the violets to the outside of the vase, or attach them to chenille "stems" and place the flowers in the vase.

Optional: Cover the jar with violet construction paper (purple) before adding the flowers.

Violet Patterns

Links to Literacy

Students can practice letter recognition, letter-sound relationship, and classification skills after making the Witch Container. Have the students fill the container with small objects and picture cutouts of things that begin with the letter **Ww**.

Materials

- small, empty soup can

- witch patterns (page 72)

- black acrylic paint

- paintbrush

- small scraps of orange and red tissue paper

- glue

- scissors

- crayons or markers

- pictures and small objects that begin with the letter **Ww**

Art Project Instructions

1. To make the witch's cauldron, paint the soup can with black acrylic paint and allow time to dry.

2. Reproduce, color, and cut out the witch patterns.

3. Glue the witch's head (Tab C) to the top back of the painted can.

4. Glue Tabs A and B of the arm pieces to the back of the container.

5. Glue scraps of orange and red tissue paper to the bottom front of the painted container to create flames around the cauldron.

Tab B

Tab A

Tab C

Links to Literacy

Students can practice letter recognition, letter-sound relationship, and classification skills after making the X-Ray Machine Container. Have the students fill the container with small objects and picture cutouts of things that begin with the letter **Xx**.

Materials

- 2 small pudding cups
- small cereal box 11.25" tall (25.6 cm)
- skeleton and person patterns (pages 74–75)
- black acrylic paint or black paper
- paintbrush
- clear cellophane or kitchen wrap
- glue and tape
- crayons or markers
- scissors
- pictures and small objects that begin with the letter **Xx**

Art Project Instructions

1. Cut the top off the cereal box.

2. On the front of the box, cut out a large rectangular shape, without cutting through to the edges.

3. Paint the inside and outside of the box with black acrylic paint (or cover it with black paper). Allow time to dry.

4. Reproduce, color, and cut out the skeleton and person patterns.

5. Glue the skeleton pattern inside the cereal box (against the back) so that it can be seen through the hole in the front of the box.

6. Tape a piece of cellophane inside the box (against the front) to cover the hole in the front. This will be the X-Ray Machine window.

7. Glue the head piece (Tab A) to the top of the back of the box, so that it appears someone is behind the box.

8. Glue the arm pieces (Tab B) to the back edges of the box, so that the arms stick out.

9. To make the leg stands for the X-Ray Machine, glue one pudding cup on each end of the bottom of the cereal box.

10. Glue the feet (Tabs C) to the bottom back of the box. You will be able to see the feet between the pudding cups.

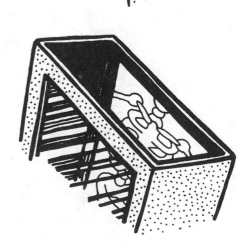

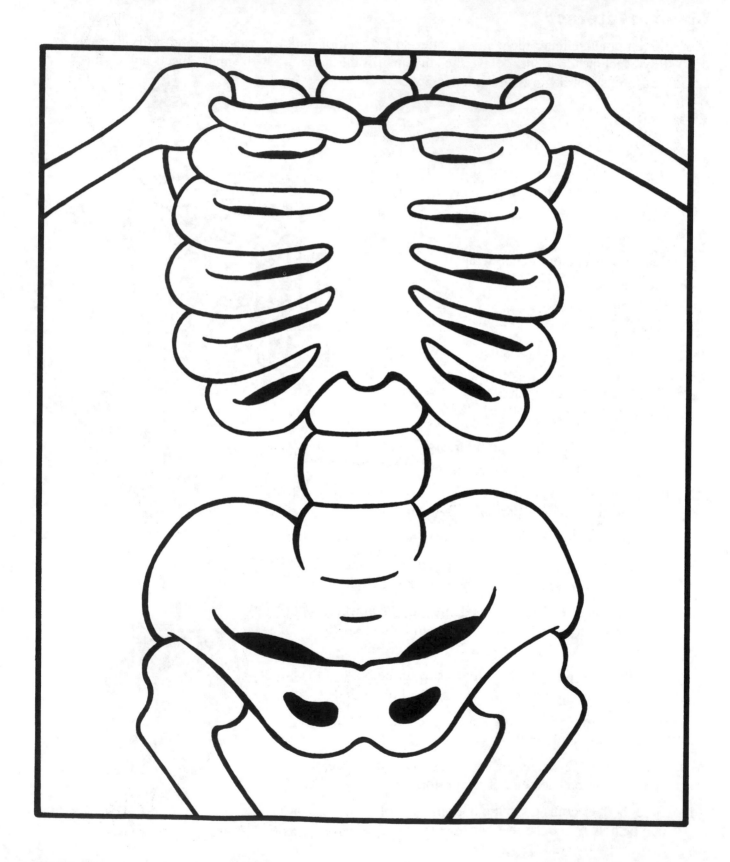

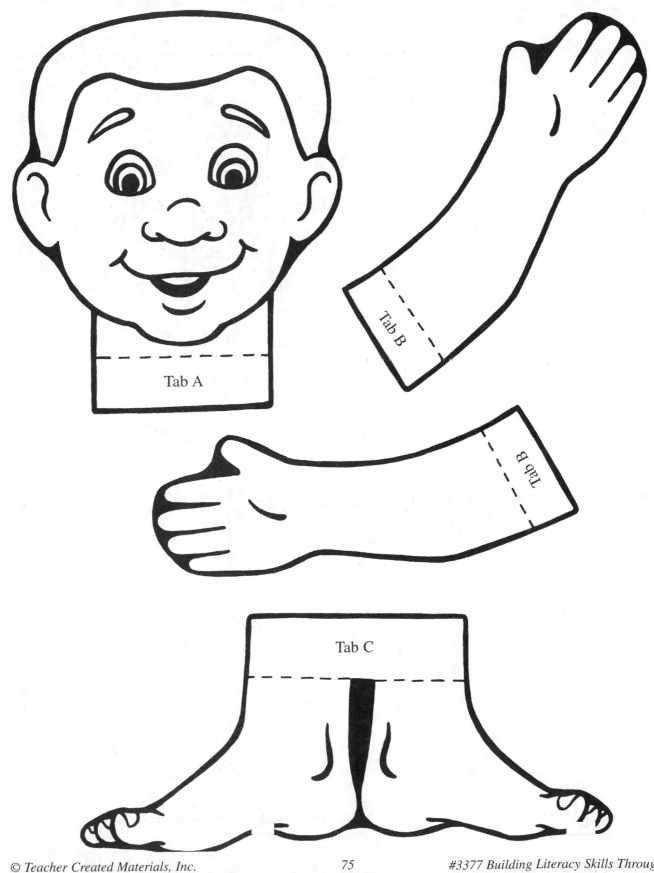

Tab A

Tab B

Tab B

Tab C

Classification Containers

Links to Literacy

Students can practice letter recognition, letter-sound relationship, and classification skills after making the Yacht Container. Have the students fill the container with small objects and picture cutouts of things that begin with the letter **Yy**.

Materials

- small milk carton (pint)
- medium-sized milk carton (quart)
- patterns (page 77)
- yellow acrylic paint or yellow paper
- paintbrush
- crayons or markers
- glue
- scissors
- pictures and small objects that begin with the letter **Yy**

Art Project Instructions

1. To make the boat, lay the medium-sized milk carton on its side and cut out half of the top side of the carton. This will be the container opening.

2. Paint both milk cartons with the yellow acrylic paint (or cover it with yellow paper) and allow time to dry. Repeat if it does not cover well enough the first time.

3. Glue the small milk carton on top of the larger milk carton, beside the cut half.

4. Reproduce, color, and cut out the yacht patterns.

5. Glue the water patterns onto the front of the yacht.

6. Glue the yacht cabin pattern around the front of the small milk carton.

7. Write the yacht's name in the nameplate. Glue the nameplate to the back of the boat.

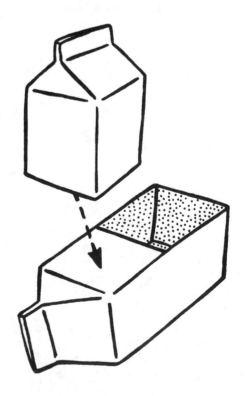

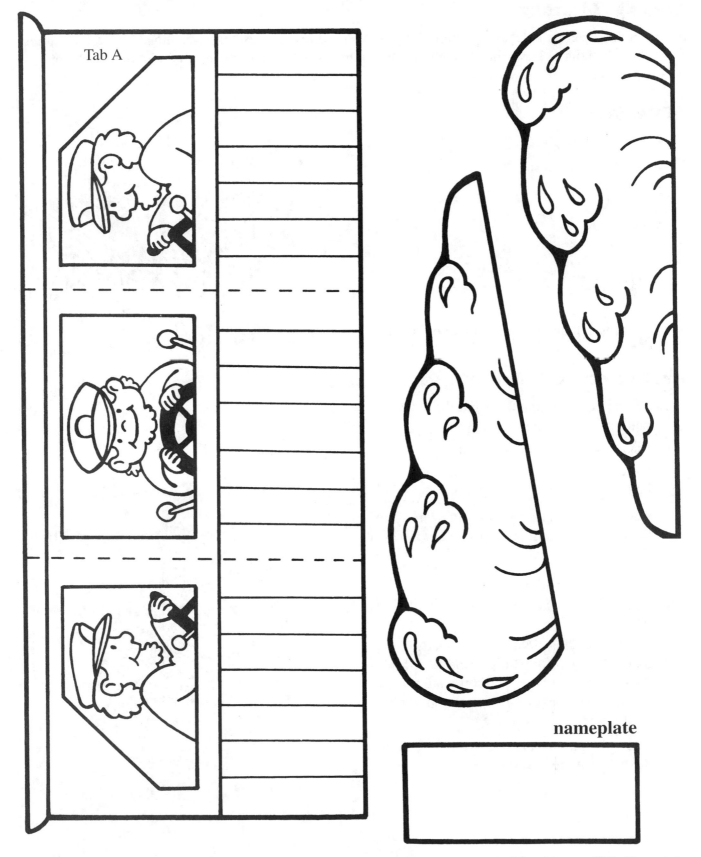

Tab A

nameplate

Classification Containers

Links to Literacy

Students can practice letter recognition, letter-sound relationship, and classification skills after making the Zebra Container. Have the students fill the container with small objects and picture cutouts of things that begin with the letter **Zz**.

Materials

- small pudding box
- zebra patterns (page 79)
- black permanent marker
- crayons or markers
- scissors
- glue
- tape
- pictures and small objects that begin with the letter **Zz**

Art Project Instructions

1. Reproduce, color, and cut out the zebra patterns.

2. Fold the body pattern along the 2 dotted lines. Glue the body over the top and sides of the box.

3. Carefully cut the gray area in the middle of the pattern, cutting through the box, to create the container opening.

4. To make the head, fold Tab A and Tab B. Glue the two heads together. Tape the head to the front end of the box.

5. To make the tail, fold the tail piece along the dotted line and fold Tabs C and D downward. Glue the tail together under the tail pieces. Apply glue atop Tabs C and D and glue the tail to the other end of the box.

6. Using the black marker, color in any parts of the box that are still showing.

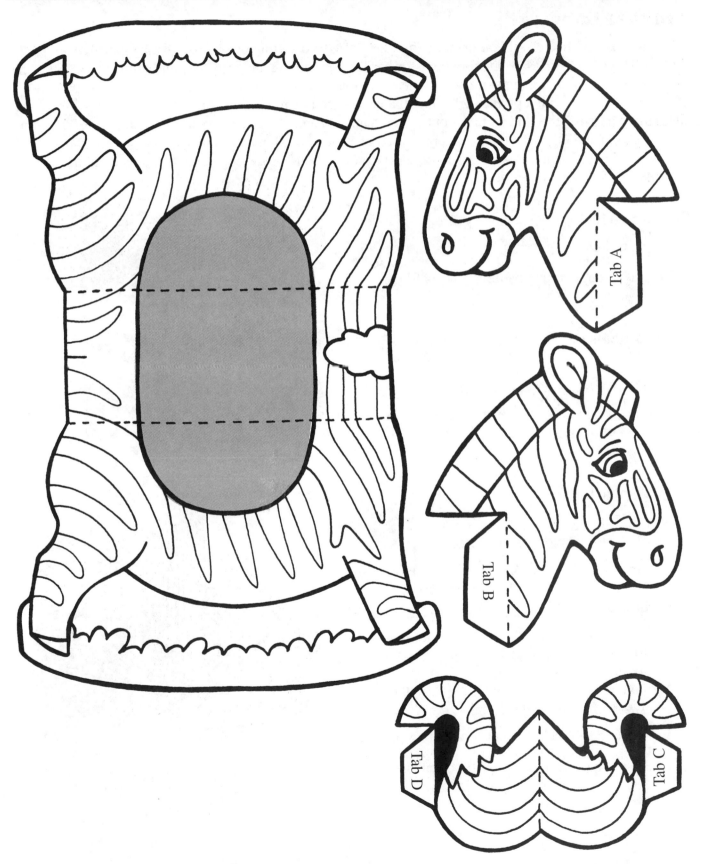

Creepy Crawly Bug Bag

Links to Literacy

Students can practice classification skills by identifying and sorting bugs after making the Creepy Crawly Bug Bag. First, a student puts his or her hand in the bag and pulls out one of the bugs. Then, he or she names the bug and puts it back in the bag. You may wish to review the pictures before playing. If you are playing with a partner or group, the next person then takes a turn picking out a bug. To extend the activity, the student picks out a bug, names it, and classifies it. All of the bugs that fly might be one group and all of the bugs that crawl could be another. Think of as many ways as you can (number of feet, antennae, stingers, color, etc.) to sort the different creepy crawlies that are in the Bug Bag.

Materials

- paper lunch bag
- plastic bugs or bug patterns (pages 81–82)
- black tempera paint
- paintbrush
- white crayons
- markers or crayons
- scissors
- glue
- aluminum foil

Art Project Instructions

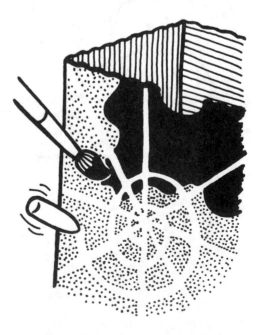

1. Draw a spider web on one side of the bag using a white crayon. Press the crayon firmly while drawing the web.

2. Paint the entire bag black and allow time to dry. (The black paint can be diluted by adding water.)

3. Cut out a spider shape from aluminum foil and glue it onto the web.

4. Reproduce, color, and cut out the bug patterns.

5. Fill the bag with bugs (plastic or paper).

Cricket, Grasshopper, Cockroach, Centipede, and Moth

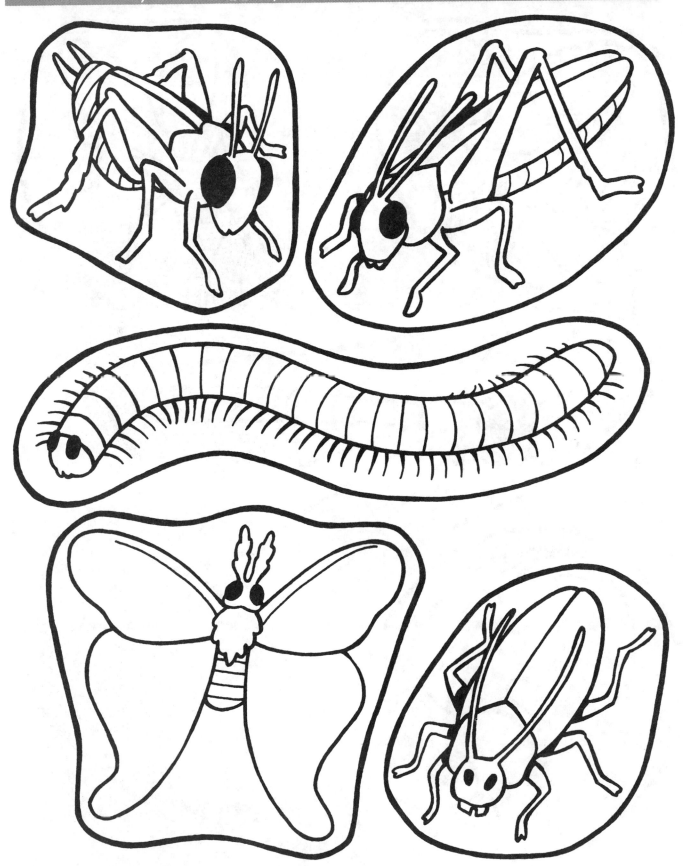

Bug Patterns (cont.)

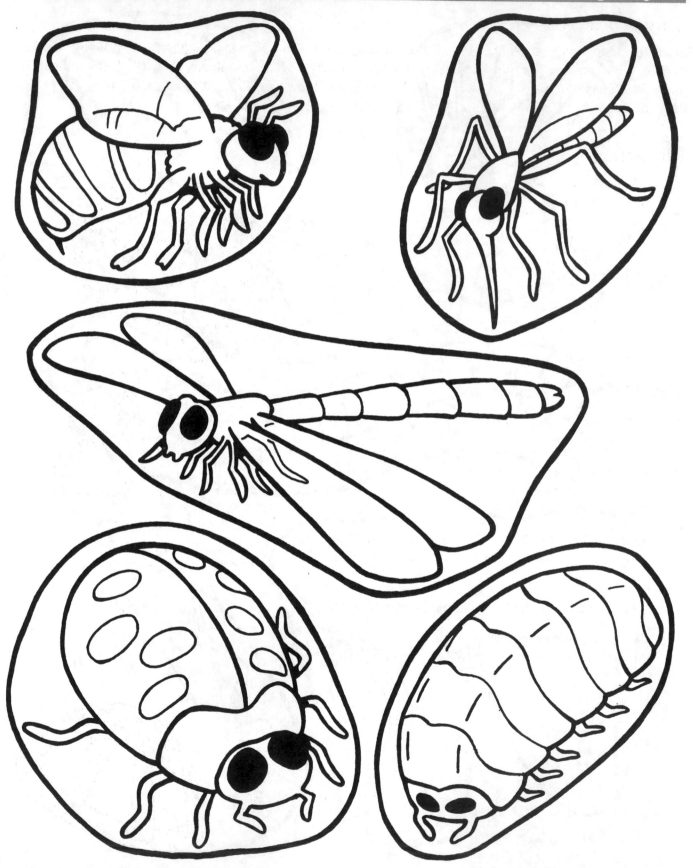

82

Objective: Classifying skills

Links to Literacy

Students can practice classification skills by identifying flowers after making the Bowl Bonnet. On the bonnet, have students use only cutouts of flowers that they have seen and can identify. Help students learn the names of common flowers, such as rose, tulip, daisy, daffodil, carnation, and pansy. To extend the activity, go on a nature walk to look for a variety of common flowers.

Materials

- 2 large paper plates
- flower patterns (page 84)
- bright-colored paints
- paintbrush
- crayons or markers
- scissors
- glue
- stapler

Art Project Instructions

1. Cut one paper plate into six equal slices, leaving the center intact.

2. Cut out the center of the second plate. Keep this "ring" facedown. Staple the edges of the first paper plate to the "ring" plate.

3. Flip the Bowl Bonnet over and paint the top of it in a rainbow of colors. Make each strip a different color,

4. Reproduce, color, and cut out the flower patterns.

5. Glue each flower to a separate strip on the Bowl Bonnet.

Flower Patterns

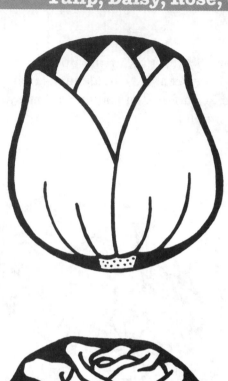

Objective: Classifying skills

Links to Literacy

Students will practice classification skills by naming and classifying a variety of animals. Pets, farm animals, wild animals, and water animals are possible categories for this activity. Categorize the animals according to the labels on the train cars. To extend the activity, brainstorm other animals that fit into each category or additional categories for animals.

Materials

- 4 individual-sized milk cartons (half pint)
- medium-sized milk carton (quart)
- train patterns (see page 86–87)
- acrylic paint or paper
- paintbrush

- crayons or markers
- pencil
- permanent marker
- scissors
- glue

- small spool
- string or yarn
- plastic farm animals
- plastic zoo animals
- plastic jungle animals

Art Project Instructions

1. Glue the milk cartons closed.

2. Paint all five cartons (or cover them with paper). Allow time to dry.

3. Reproduce, color, and cut out the train patterns.

4. To make the engine, lay the medium-sized carton on its side. Glue an individual-sized carton on top, at the back. Glue the spool in the front on top. Glue the engine patterns onto the sides of the larger carton (bottom) and the window pieces to the smaller carton (top).

5. To make the train cars, glue the colored pattern pieces to the sides of two individual-sized cartons. Glue the caboose patterns to the sides of the last individual-sized carton.

6. With a sharpened pencil, carefully punch a hole through each side of each car of the train and run the string through all the cartons, tying a knot at each end.

7. Using a permanent marker, label each train car with a different category of animals.

Train Patterns

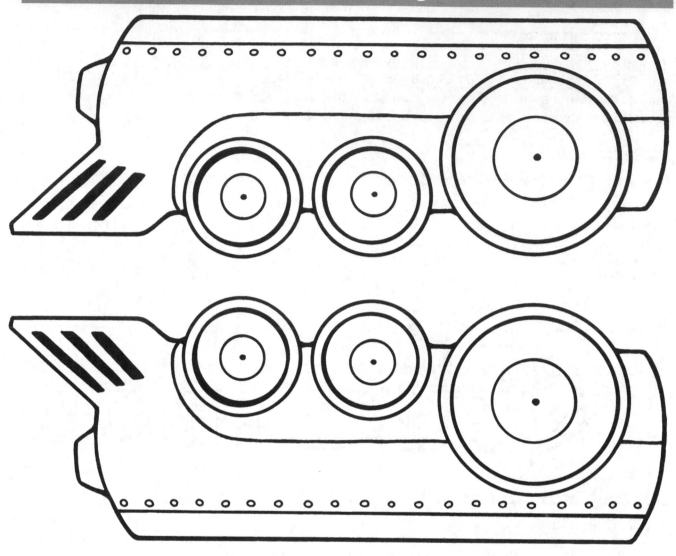

86

Train Cars and Caboose

Color Classification

Links to Literacy

Students can practice identifying colors and color combinations by placing a small object or picture cutout into a tub representing a certain color. Each object or picture can be introduced and shared with the class before putting it into one of the color containers. To extend the activity, discuss what combinations of colors create other colors.

Materials

- baby wipes containers in a variety of colors
- colored paper
- crayons or markers
- scissors
- tape or glue
- old magazines or small objects in a variety of colors

Art Project Instructions

1. Place students in groups and assign each group a color. Give that group a baby wipes container of that color.

2. Remove any stickers or labels from the container.

3. Cut out a small rectangular label of the assigned color. Tape or glue the color label onto the appropriate container.

4. Draw and cut out a picture of something that is a certain color and glue it to the lid of the container representing that color (for example, red—apple, green—leaf).

5. Cut out pictures from old magazines of items that are of the assigned color.

6. Place the pictures in the box.

1-2-3-4-5 Fishing Rod

Links to Literacy

Once I Caught a Fish Alive

1-2-3-4-5, Once I caught a fish alive,
6-7-8-9-10, Then I let it go again.
Why did you let it go?
Because it bit my finger so.
Which finger did it bite?
This little finger on the right.

Place emphasis on the rhyming words as "Once I Caught a Fish Alive" is recited. Hook a sea creature on the fishing rod using the egg carton cup as bait and the magnet as a hook. With each creature you catch, recite the rhyme, changing the word *fish* to match your picture. Example: 1-2-3-4-5, Once I caught an "octopus" alive.

Materials

- paper clips
- 1' (30 cm) length of string
- 2 sheets of white construction paper
- paper towel tube
- sea creature patterns (pages 90–91)
- egg carton cup
- bright-colored acrylic paint
- paintbrush
- crayons or markers
- pencil
- scissors
- tape
- donut magnet

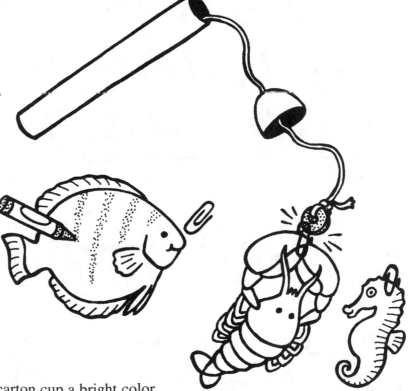

Art Project Instructions

1. Paint the paper-towel tube and egg carton cup a bright color.
2. Tape one end of the string to the inside of the tube.
3. Poke a small hole in the bottom of the egg carton cup using a sharpened pencil. Push the free end of the string through the small hole and tie a magnet to the end.
4. Reproduce the sea creature patterns onto the white construction paper. Color the patterns and cut them out. (If possible, laminate the sea creatures.)
5. Attach a paper clip to each sea creature and arrange them in a bowl or other assigned area.

Sea Creature Patterns

Sea Turtle, Octopus, Sea Horse, and Lobster

Tube Spout and Spider

Links to Literacy

Itsy Bitsy Spider

The itsy bitsy spider climbed up the waterspout,
Down came the rain and washed the spider out.
Out came the sun and dried up all the rain,
And the itsy bitsy spider climbed up the spout again.

Place emphasis on the rhyming words as "Itsy Bitsy Spider" is recited. Lower the spider down the tube while holding the top of the string. Keep playing with the spider and spout (tube), pulling the spider up or moving it down and out, while saying the rhyme.

Materials

- 2 toilet paper tubes

- 4 black chenille sticks

- small black pompom

- tape

- string

Art Project Instructions

1. To create the water spout, gently push in the end of one toilet paper tube so that it slides into the other tube (about 1"). Bend the tubes to give the spout a slight angle; then fasten them together with tape.

2. Create a small spider by wrapping a black chenille stick around the black pompom and twisting the chenille stick to keep it in place. Each stick will make two of the spider legs. Repeat with three more chenille sticks so that the spider has eight legs.

3. Tie some string to one of the black chenille sticks that is in the middle of the spider's body.

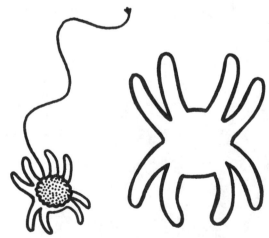

Variation: Attach the pompom to the pattern of legs given on this page if the little hands doing the project have difficulty with coordination.

Objective: Recognizing rhymes

Links to Literacy

The Wheels on the Bus
The wheels on the bus go round and round,
Round and round, round and round.
The wheels on the bus go round and round,
All through the town.

Place emphasis on the rhyming words as "The Wheels on the Bus" is recited. Students can play with their buses and make the wheels go round and round while they sing or recite the verse. For each additional verse, substitute another part of the bus (i.e., wipers).

Materials

- 2 toilet paper tubes
- paper fasteners (brads)
- 2 sheets of yellow construction paper
- tissue box
- bus patterns (page 94)
- tagboard
- scissors
- glue
- tape
- cardboard (optional)

Art Project Instructions

1. Cut the top off the tissue box and turn the box over, so that the bottom of the box makes the top of the bus.

2. To form the hood of the bus, tape the two toilet paper tubes together; then place them in front of the tissue box. Join the box and the tubes together with tape.

3. Using glue, cover the bus with yellow construction paper. Don't cover the bottom of the bus.

4. Reproduce and cut out the bus windows and tires.

5. Glue the large window to the front of the bus. On each side, glue three windows close to the top.

6. Carefully poke a paper fastener into the center of each tire; then attach the tires to the bottom of each side of the bus. Close the fasteners inside the tissue box by using the bottom end (uncovered) of the box. (**Note:** You may wish to glue the tire patterns onto cardboard before attaching them to the bus.)

7. Cut out two small strips of tagboard to make windshield wipers. Attach each to the large window using a paper fastener.

Bus Patterns

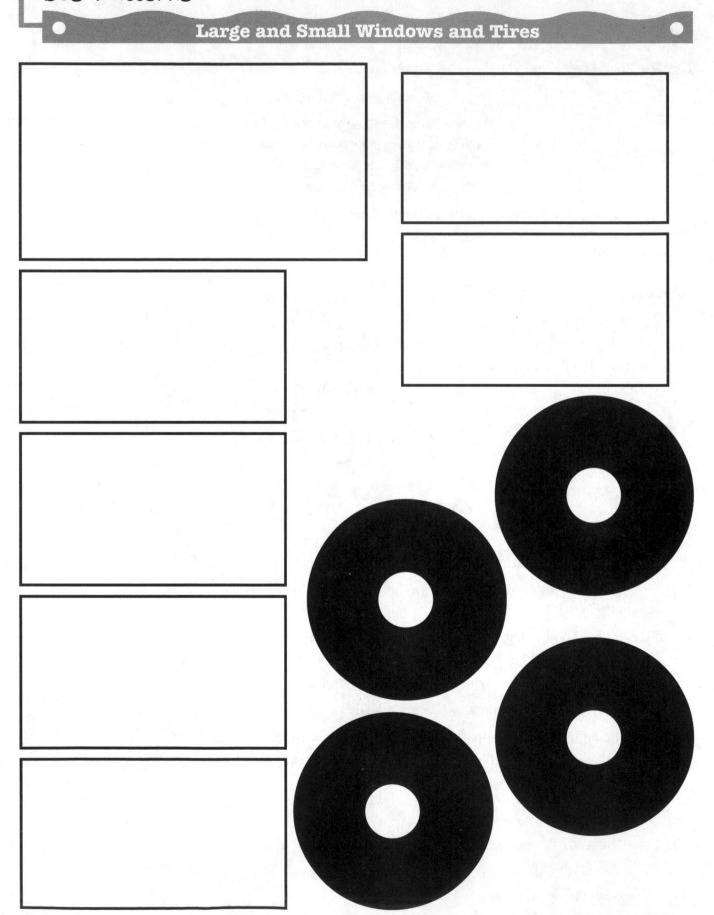

94

Links to Literacy

Little Boy Blue

Little Boy Blue, come blow your horn,
The sheep's in the meadow, the cow's in the corn.
Where is the boy who looks after the sheep?
He's under the haystack, fast asleep.

Place emphasis on the rhyming words as "Little Boy Blue" is recited. Students can pretend to blow their horns to wake up Boy Blue. Students can also pretend that Boy Blue is finally awake and herding the sheep and cows back to their places. To extend the activity, discuss farm life and farm animals.

Materials

- 3 jumbo craft sticks
- toilet paper tube
- small Styrofoam cup
- Boy Blue patterns (page 96)
- acrylic paint
- paintbrush
- sheet of white construction paper
- crayons or markers
- tape
- scissors
- thick string

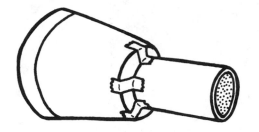

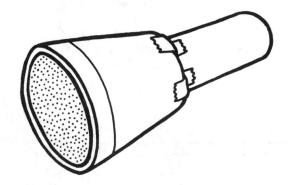

Art Project Instructions

1. Cut a hole in the bottom of the Styrofoam cup the same size as the end of the toilet paper tube.

2. Fit the toilet paper tube into the hole and tape it in place.

3. Paint the horn and allow time to dry.

4. Make a loose string handle for the horn by taping the string onto the tube, or by poking holes in the sides and running the string through the cup.

5. Reproduce the Boy Blue patterns onto the white construction paper. Color the patterns and cut them out.

6. Tape a craft stick onto the back of each pattern to create a stick puppet.

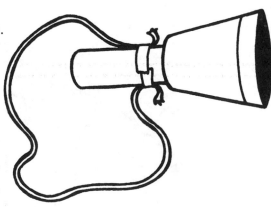

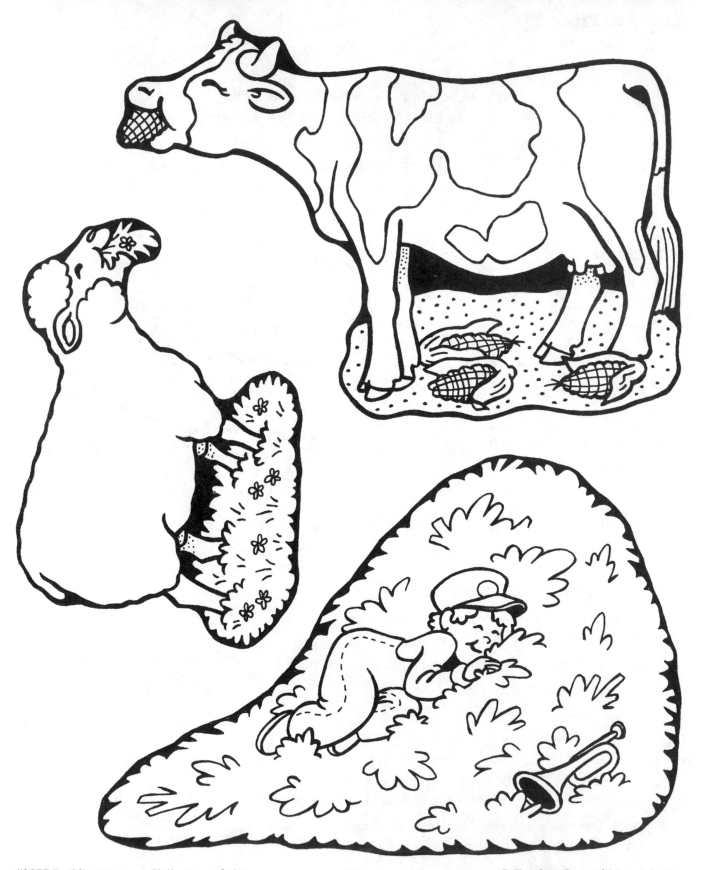

Links to Literacy

Old Mother Hubbard

Old Mother Hubbard went to her cupboard,
To fetch her poor dog a bone,
But when she got there,
The cupboard was bare,
And so the poor dog had none.

Place emphasis on the rhyming words as "Old Mother Hubbard" is recited. After making the Mother Hubbard and dog stick puppets, use them to act out the verse. To extend the activity, discuss how people help each other in our communities and in other countries when people don't have enough food. Cut out foods from old magazines to stock Old Mother Hubbard's cupboard.

Materials

- 2 egg cartons
- 2 jumbo craft sticks
- Old Mother Hubbard patterns (page 98)
- acrylic paint
- paintbrush
- sheet of white construction paper
- crayons or markers
- scissors
- tape
- old magazines

Art Project Instructions

1. Cut the lids off the egg cartons. Set aside the two egg cup trays and one top.
2. Cut one lid in half.
3. Place the two lid tops opened up, side by side, and tape them together by pressing the tape over the rims in the middle.
4. Close the lids together, then open and shut them again so that the tape is not too stiff. This will be the cupboard that can be opened and closed.
5. Cut out rectangular shelves from the remaining lid and tape the shelves in place on the inside of one of the cupboard lids.
6. Paint the inside and outside of the cupboard and allow time to dry.
7. Reproduce the Old Mother Hubbard patterns onto the white construction paper. Color the patterns and cut them out.
8. Tape a craft stick to the back of each pattern to create a stick puppet.

Links to Literacy

Traffic Lights

"Stop," says the red light.
"Go," says the green.
"Wait," says the yellow light, blinking in between.

Place emphasis on the rhyming words as "Traffic Lights" is recited. Point to the correct color on the Traffic Lights with each line that is said. Students can point to their traffic lights and tell what each color means: *stop, go,* or *wait*. To extend the activity, play the game, "Red Light, Green Light," and point to each color when the corresponding word is said.

Materials

- 3 rubber bands

- egg carton

- black acrylic paint

- paintbrushes

- pencils

- scissors

- glue gun

- red, yellow, and green cellophane or plastic wrap

Art Project Instructions

1. Separate the lid of the egg carton from the egg carton cups.

2. Completely paint the outside of the lid black and allow time to dry.

3. Cut out three egg carton cups.

4. Cover one egg cup with red cellophane and secure a rubber band around the hollow side so it stays in place. Do the same with the remaining two cups, but use yellow cellophane to cover one, and green cellophane to cover the other.

5. Using a pencil, trace three circles onto the yellow painted lid to use as a guide.

6. Glue the red cup onto the top circle, the yellow cup onto the middle, and the green cup onto the bottom circle.

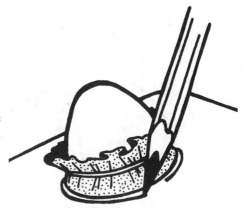

Teacup

Links to Literacy

I'm a Little Teapot

I'm a little teapot, short and stout,
Here is my handle and here is my spout.
When I get all steamed up, hear me shout,
Tip me over and pour me out.

Place emphasis on the rhyming words as "I'm a Little Teapot" is recited. When tipping over to pour the tea out, students can pretend to fill their teacups.

Materials

- 2 egg carton cups
- scissors
- glue
- pencil
- chenille stick

Art Project Instructions

1. Cut one egg carton cup in half horizontally.

2. Glue the bottoms of the two egg carton cups together, using the cut cup as the base of the teacup.

3. Using a chenille stick, create a handle for the teacup.

4. Using a sharpened pencil, gently poke one small hole into the top and bottom of the egg carton cup that has not been cut.

5. Insert each end of the handle into a hole to finish the teacup.

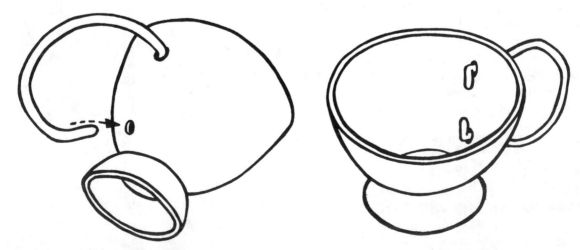

Paper Plate Pumpkin Play

Links to Literacy

Peter, Peter, Pumpkin Eater

Peter, Peter, Pumpkin Eater
Had a wife and couldn't keep her.
He put her in a pumpkin shell
And there he kept her very well.

Place emphasis on the rhyming words as "Peter, Peter, Pumpkin Eater" is recited. Have children chant the nursery rhyme while playing with the Paper Plate Pumpkins.

Materials

- large white paper plate
- Peter Pumpkin patterns (page 102)
- orange acrylic paint
- paintbrush
- crayons or markers
- scissors
- glue

Art Project Instructions

1. Paint the back of the plate orange, and allow time for it to dry.

2. Cut one triangle window out of the middle of the plate.

3. Reproduce, color, and cut out the Peter Pumpkin patterns.

4. Glue Peter to the outside of the plate; then glue his wife to the inside, looking out the window. Glue the pumpkin stem to the top of the plate.

Variation: Staple another paper plate to the back of the paper plate to hold Peter's wife inside.

Peter Pumpkin Patterns

Objective: Recognizing rhymes

Links to Literacy

There Was an Old Woman

There was an old woman who lived in a shoe,
She had so many children, she didn't know what to do.
She gave them some broth, without any bread,
And kissed them all soundly and sent them to bed.

Place emphasis on the rhyming words as "There Was an Old Woman" is recited. Have the students place the patterns of the Old Woman's children inside the shoe to put them to bed. Then have them count how many children are in the shoe.

Materials

- 1' (30 cm) length of yarn
- shoebox
- oatmeal container
- Old Woman and Children patterns (page 104)
- brown construction paper
- crayons or markers
- scissors
- glue

Art Project Instructions

1. Cover the shoebox and oatmeal tube with brown construction paper.

2. Shape the yarn into a tied shoelace bow and glue it onto the tube. Draw on criss-crossed laces.

3. Draw windows on the tube and box.

4. Draw a door.

5. Glue the tube to the top of one end of the shoebox, with the shoelace facing the long end of the box. This forms the shoe.

6. Reproduce, color, and cut out the Old Woman and Children patterns.

Old Woman and Children

Links to Literacy

There Was a Little Turtle

There was a little turtle, he lived in a box.
He swam in a puddle, he climbed on the rocks.
He snapped at a mosquito, he snapped at a flea.
He snapped at a minnow, and he snapped at me.
He caught the mosquito, he caught the flea.
He caught the minnow, but he didn't catch me!

Place emphasis on the rhyming words as "There Was a Little Turtle" is recited. While saying the poem, each student puts two fingers into his or her Little Turtle and moves the turtle around. Then, he or she places the turtle in a box, on the puddle, and on a rock. Finally, have the turtle catch the mosquito, the flea, and the minnow, and turn the turtle toward the student.

Materials

- toilet paper tube
- Little Turtle patterns (page 106)
- scissors
- glue or tape
- blue paper
- crayons or markers
- rock
- small box

Art Project Instructions

1. Reproduce, color, and cut out the turtle shell and body patterns.

2. Use glue or tape to attach the turtle shell and body to the toilet paper tube.

3. Cut out a sloppy circle from the blue paper to make a pond.

4. Cut out and color the minnow, the flea, and the mosquito.

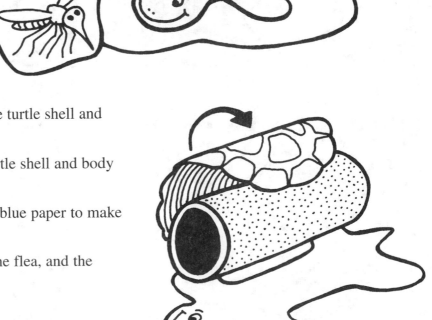

Little Turtle Patterns

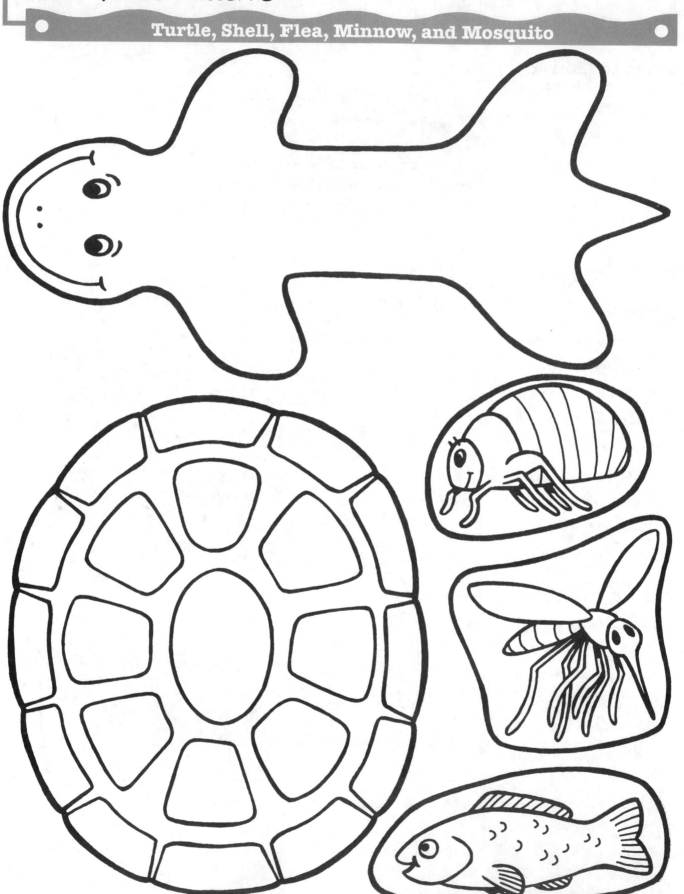

106

Objective: Recognizing rhymes

Links to Literacy

Tom, Tom, the Piper's Son

Tom, Tom, the piper's son,
Stole a pig and away he run!
The pig was eat. Tom was beat,
And Tom went roaring down the street.

Place emphasis on the rhyming words as "Tom, Tom, the Piper's Son" is recited. Choral read the rhyme while different students take turns acting out grabbing the Poor Pig. To extend the activity, have a discussion on good and bad behavior, focusing on what we should and shouldn't do. Should Tom have done what he did?

Materials

- 2 toilet paper tubes
- paper lunch bag
- Poor Pig patterns (page 108)
- pink acrylic paint
- paintbrush
- sheet of pink construction paper
- scissors
- glue and tape
- newspaper or paper towel

Art Project Instructions

1. Cut each of the two toilet paper tubes in half to make four pig feet. Cut a small wedge in one side of each foot.

2. Scrunch up newspaper and stuff the paper bag until is is almost full. Fold the open end closed and secure it with tape to form the body of the pig.

3. Paint the paper bag and toilet paper tubes pink. Allow time to dry.

4. Attach the legs to the pig using tape.

5. Reproduce the Poor Pig patterns onto pink construction paper; then cut them out.

6. Glue the face to one end of the bag and fold the pig's ears downward. Attach the tail to the opposite end of the bag.

Pig Head and Tail

Tab A

Links to Literacy

Humpty Dumpty

Humpty Dumpty sat on a wall;
Humpty Dumpty had a great fall.
All the King's horses and all the King's men
Couldn't put Humpty together again.

Place emphasis on the rhyming words as "Humpty Dumpty" is recited. Place Humpty Dumpty on top of the brick wall box. Recite the rhyme and give him a slight push so he falls off the wall. To extend the activity, have students put Humpty Dumpty in a variety of locations. Have them use prepositional phrases to describe the location—on, under, over, in, etc.

Materials

- egg carton cup
- small box
- Humpty Dumpty patterns (page 110)
- sheet of red construction paper
- crayons or markers
- scissors
- glue
- tape
- chenille stick

Art Project Instructions

1. Reproduce, color, and cut out the Humpty Dumpty patterns. To make Humpty Dumpty, glue the body pattern to the front of the upside down egg carton cup.

2. Cut the chenille stick into two pieces. Glue the middle of one stick to the top of the egg carton cup to make his arms, and push the other stick in one side and out the other to make his legs.

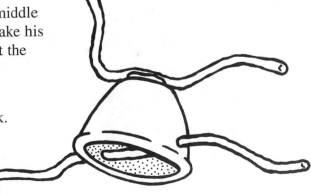

3. Tape one hand to each of the top chenille sticks (from the back) and one foot to each bottom stick.

4. Using glue, cover the box with red construction paper.

5. Draw small rectangles on the red paper to make bricks.

Humpty Dumpty Patterns

Links to Literacy

Students can develop their recognition of numbers and counting skills by playing with the Domino Sticks they have created. Students take turns laying down a Domino Stick and matching it up with the correct number of happy faces on another stick. To extend the activity, label each stick with a word number instead of using the happy faces. This way students will have to read and recognize the words and the numbers.

Materials

- 10 jumbo craft sticks

- yellow acrylic paint

- paintbrush

- black permanent marker

Art Project Instructions

1. Paint all of the craft sticks yellow. Allow time to dry.

2. Line up the craft sticks in front of you, and on one end of each craft stick, print a number (from 1–10).

3. Draw happy faces on the other end of each craft stick (from 1–10). Do not draw the same number of happy faces on the stick with that numeral on it, or you will be unable to match this Domino Stick.

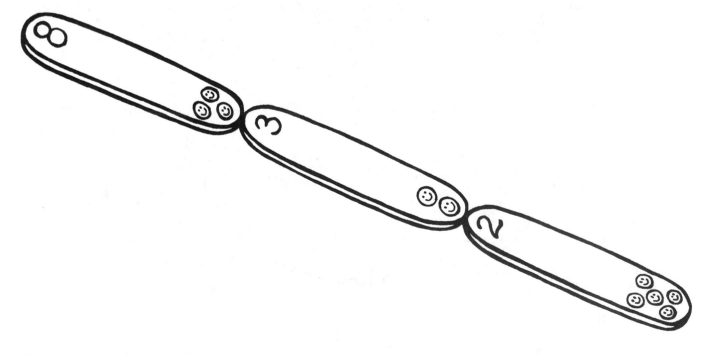

Equestrian Jumping Course

Links to Literacy

Students can build number sense skills after creating the Equestrian Jumping Course. Have each student develop his or her own set of points per obstacle in the jumping course. Advise students to give each obstacle a rating from 1–10. Use stick puppets, small pets, or toy animals to run the course. One person can be the judge to call out the number of points given during a run.

Materials

- 4 paper towel tubes
- 6 drinking straws
- jumbo craft stick
- horse pattern (page 113)
- blue and red construction paper
- crayons or markers
- scissors
- glue
- tape
- hole punch
- small box

Art Project Instructions

1. Cut two paper towel tubes, ⅓ of the way down, so that you have two each of three sizes of tubes.

2. Punch three holes in the tallest tubes, two holes in the middle-sized tubes, and one hole in the shortest toilet paper tubes.

3. Insert the straws into the holes so that the straw is balanced in between the two tubes of the same size. The shortest tubes will only have one straw while the remaining tubes will have two and three straws.

4. Glue red paper over the small box to cover it. Draw brick shapes onto the paper. This will create a brick wall for the jumping course.

5. Cut out an uneven circular shape from the blue construction paper. Use the paper to create a large water pond or puddle.

6. Reproduce, color, and cut out the horse pattern. Tape a craft stick to the back of the horse to create a stick puppet for the course.

7. Lay out the course on a flat surface.

Burger Box Game

Links to Literacy

Students can practice counting skills from 1–10. Each of the 10 burger boxes contains one number (from 1–10). Mix up the boxes, and with a partner, in a group, or alone, choose a burger box and open it up. Numbers need to be found in order, with one being first. If you open up a correct box, pull the burger number out and place it in front of you and try again for the next number needed. If you open up the wrong box, close it, and put it back with the others. Keep trying until you get the right box. The person to get the last box with the number 10 wins.

Materials

- 10 small Styrofoam takeout containers with lids

- 2 sheets of white construction paper

- hamburger patterns (page 115)

- scissors

- crayons or markers

Art Project Instructions

1. Reproduce the hamburger patterns onto white construction paper. Color the patterns and cut them out. For each game, make 10 hamburgers.

2. On the top of each burger bun, print a number (from 1–10).

3. Place each completed hamburger inside a box and close the lid.

Crazy Quills Porcupine

Links to Literacy

Students can polish their skip counting skills while creating Crazy Quills Porcupines. Encourage the students to count the quills they put on the bodies. Suggest a specific number of quills that each porcupine body should have. Students should easily be able to find room for 50 quills if that is the number you would like them to count up to. To extend the activity, have students count by 2's or 5's in counting the quills they have put on the porcupines.

Materials

- 3 brown chenille sticks
- egg carton cup
- brown acrylic paint
- paintbrush
- large brown pompom
- silver glitter glue
- glue
- scissors

Art Project Instructions

1. Paint the egg carton cup brown and allow time to dry.

2. Glue the brown pompom to the front of the egg cup to create the head of the porcupine.

3. With silver glitter glue, put two eyes and a nose on the front of the pompom head.

4. If you want the porcupine to have 25 quills, cut the brown chenille sticks into twenty-five 1" (2.54 cm) pieces.

5. Use the silver glitter glue to place 25 small dots on the egg cup body of the porcupine. Gently press each of the chenille sticks into the center of a glue dot. (Make sure the chenille sticks poke through the egg carton cup. This will give the quills more stability.)

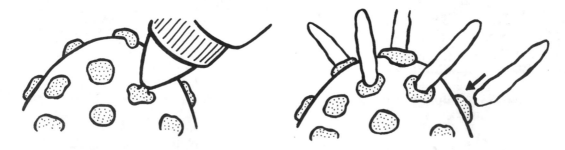

Objective: Building math skills and vocabulary

Links to Literacy

Students can review their knowledge of telling time and the vocabulary associated with it after making the Cuckoo Carton Clock. In relation to time, there are many words that students need to learn and understand. Discuss words such as o'clock, noon, midnight, half-past, quarter to, quarter after, a.m., and p.m. Review the numbers up to 12 and review skip counting by 5's up to 60.

Materials

- individual sized milk carton (half-pint)

- cuckoo clock patterns (page 118)

- acrylic paint or paper

- paintbrush

- crayons or markers

- scissors

- glue

Art Project Instructions

1. Glue the spout on the opened carton back into its original position.

2. Paint the carton (or cover it) and allow time to dry.

3. Reproduce, color, and cut out the cuckoo clock patterns.

4. Glue the bird triangle over a triangle part of the carton.

5. For the clock piece, fold along the dotted line facing down. Apply glue to Tab A and place the clock piece atop the bird piece. This creates a flap that can cover the bird, or expose it when the flap is opened.

6. Fold the roof piece along the dotted line and glue it atop the milk carton, near the front.

7. To make the chimes, fold Tab B under and glue it to the bottom of the carton.

8. Set the clock on the edge of a shelf or table to allow the chimes to hang down.

Cuckoo Clock Patterns

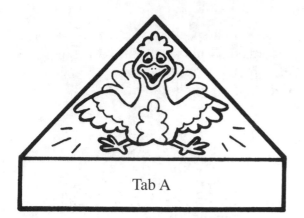

Tab A

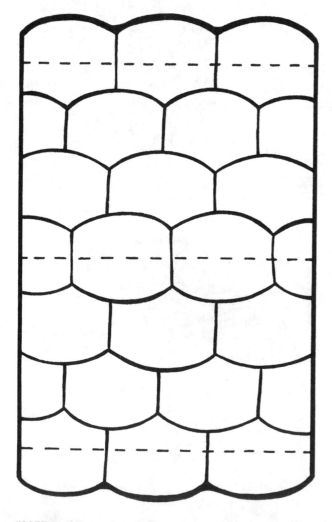

Tab B

118

Decorative Flower Clock

Links to Literacy

Students can review telling time and related time vocabulary (such as o'clock, half-past, quarter to, and quarter past), after making the Decorative Flower Clock. Have students move the hands on the paper plate clock to various times of the day. Use the rhyme, "Hickory, Dickory Dock," to give students different times to show on their clocks.

Materials

- 3 sheets of white construction paper
- large white paper plate
- flower and clock patterns (page 120)
- green construction paper
- bright-colored acrylic paint
- paintbrush
- crayons or markers
- scissors
- glue
- permanent black marker
- paper fastener
- cardboard

Art Project Instructions

1. Paint the paper plate a bright color. Allow time to dry.

2. Use a black marker to write numbers from 1–12 around the plate to create the clock face.

3. Reproduce the flower and clock patterns three times onto white construction paper.

4. Color and cut out one big hand and one small hand and attach them to the middle of the plate with a paper fastener. (You may wish to glue the hands to cardboard or laminate them for durability.)

5. Cut out a long green construction-paper stem and glue it to the plate below the number 6.

6. Color and cut out the 12 flower petals and glue them around the plate along the outside of the numbers.

7. Cut out two green construction paper leaves and glue them to the stem of the Decorative Flower Clock.

Flower and Clock Patterns

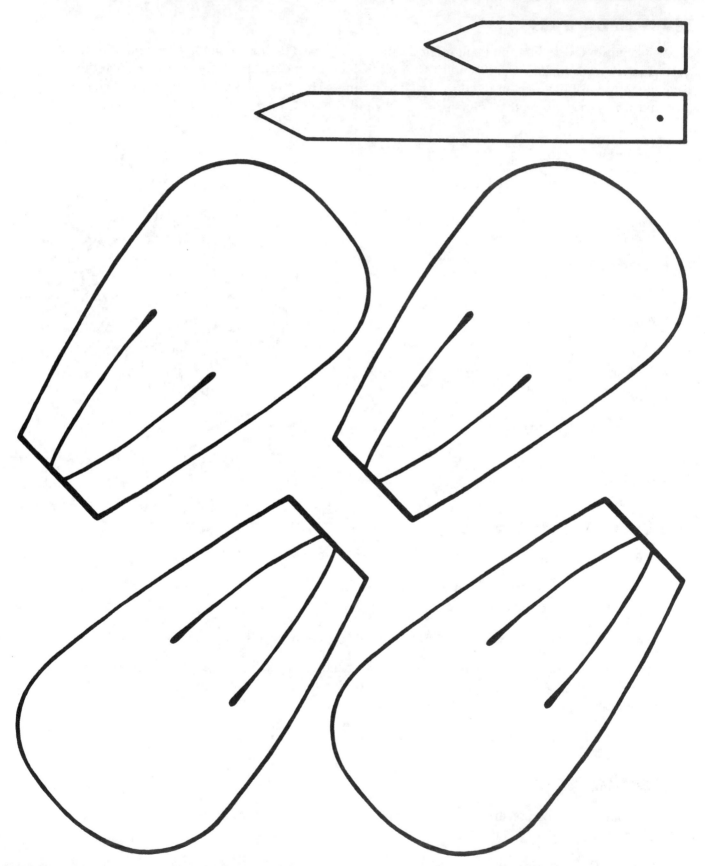

Objective: Building math skills and vocabulary

Links to Literacy

Students can practice counting and number recognition skills as they label their pushpin points for the Box Dot-to-Dot activity. Use your discretion to decide how many numbers students should have in their dot-to-dot pictures. Have students count again as they connect the pushpins points together with string. To extend the activity, have each student create a dot-to-dot of a certain shape, such as a star or an octagon to work on shape recognition skills.

Materials

- thick cardboard box
- dot-to-dot pattern (page 122)
- acrylic paint
- paintbrush
- paper
- pencil
- pushpins
- string
- scissors
- permanent marker

Art Project Instructions

1. Decide on a type of picture you would like to create as a dot-to-dot or reproduce and cut out the dot-to-dot pattern provided.

2. Use a pencil to draw the picture without any dots; then cut out the drawing.

3. Paint the box the color the picture could be and allow time to dry.

4. Put your cutout picture on the box and press in the pushpins around different points of the picture to show the outline.

5. Above or beside each pin, use a permanent marker to label numbers in sequential order to create the dot-to-dot picture.

6. Give your dot-to-dot picture and some string to a friend and have him or her put the string around the pins to create the picture outline. Tie the string around the first pin and wind it around the other pins in order.

Dot-to-Dot Pattern

122

Objective: Building math skills and vocabulary

Links to Literacy

Students can develop shape recognition and identification skills while making Tri-Angels. Refer to each shape by name when cutting it out, decorating it, or putting it in the proper place. Focus on the three sides of the triangles and the circular shape of the face, nose, and eyes, along with the oval mouth. To extend the activity, label each shape on the back of the angel using a marker or pen.

Materials

- egg carton lid

- yellow acrylic paint

- paintbrush

- construction paper

- pencil

- scissors

- glue

- tape

- gold chenille stick

Art Project Instructions

1. Paint the egg carton lid yellow and allow time to dry.

2. From the painted lid, cut out two smaller triangle shapes, one larger triangle, and one small oval.

3. Using the larger triangle piece as the body of the angel; glue one triangle piece to each side of the larger piece to create the arms.

4. Make a circle nose, two circle eyes, and an oval singing mouth from construction paper and glue it to the oval face.

5. Glue the head to the top of the body.

6. Make a circular halo from the gold chenille stick and attach it to the top of the angel's head with a small piece of tape at the back.

Crocodile Cups

Links to Literacy

Students can review counting from 1–12 after making Crocodile Cups. Alone, or with a friend, a student tosses his or her beans into the Crocodile Cups and tries to get each bean in the correct order. As he or she tosses, the student should count aloud. If the student is playing with a friend, the next student takes a turn if the bean goes into the wrong cup. Should the student be successful getting the bean in the "cup," he or she takes another turn and tries to get the next bean in the container." To extend the activity, have students put the correct number of beans into each cup, for example, three beans in the "3-cup."

Materials

- egg carton
- crocodile patterns (page 125–126)
- green acrylic paint
- paintbrush
- black permanent marker
- crayons or markers
- scissors
- glue

Art Project Instructions

1. Cut off the lid of the egg carton. This activity will use only the cup section.

2. Paint the egg carton with green acrylic paint and allow time to dry.

3. Reproduce, color, and cut out the crocodile patterns.

4. Fold the crocodile head in half. Fold Tabs A and B out. Apply glue under Tabs A and B and glue the head to one end of the carton.

5. Glue two legs, as shown, to each side of the carton.

6. Fold the sides of the tail downward along each of the dotted lines. Fold Tabs C under and apply glue to them. Glue the tail to the other end of the carton.

7. Using a permanent marker, print a number (from 1–12) on each of the egg cups on the crocodile's body.

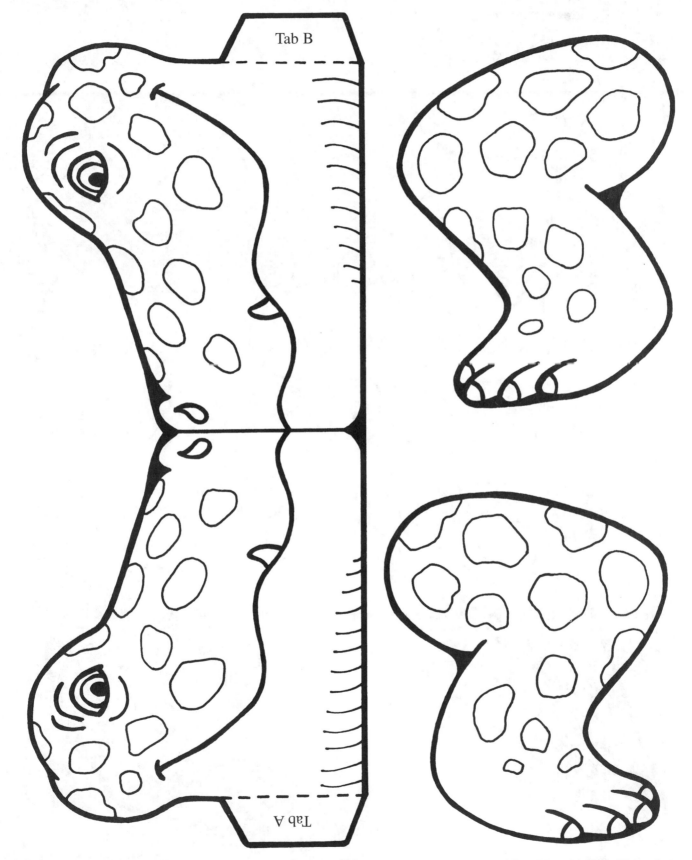

Tab B

Tab A

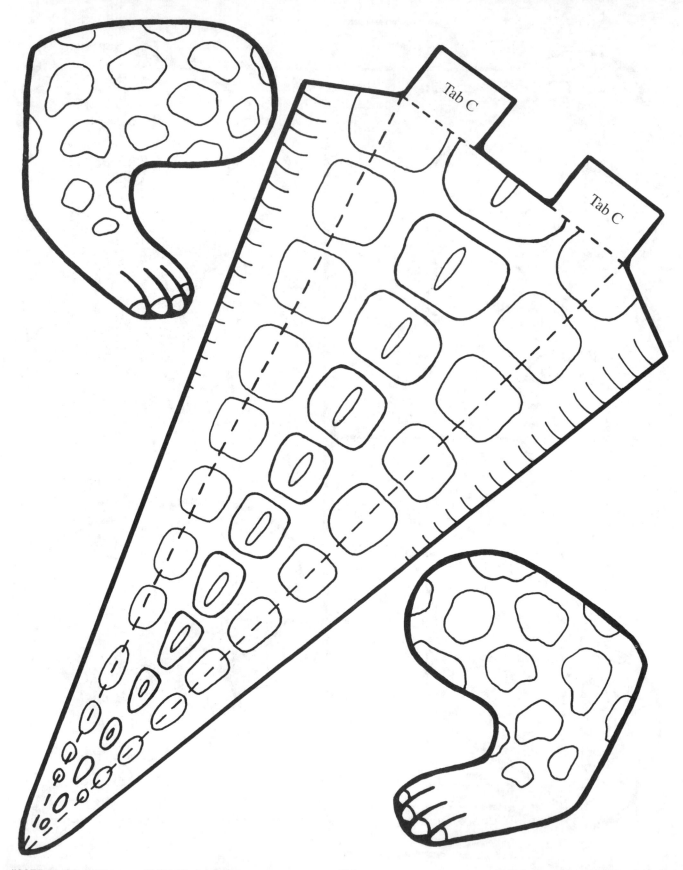

Tab C

Tab C

126

Cowboy Number Cardholder

Links to Literacy

Students can practice reading math facts and recognizing numbers and totals quickly. This activity will give them lots of individual practice. The Cowboy Number Cardholder will hold cards that will help them practice their speed or "quickness to the draw" with math vocabulary, problem solving and/or number recognition skills. Make different cards as skills improve. To extend the activity, have students make their own cards with numbers, number words, domino dots to count, or basic addition and subtractions facts.

Materials

- small plastic ketchup container
- cowboy and card patterns (pages 128–129)
- crayons or markers
- sharp scissors
- glue

Art Project Instructions

1. Cut the top off the ketchup bottle and cut out the two small sides of the container to look like a napkin holder. Only the bottom, front, and back sides should remain. (**Safety Note:** This part of the activity should be done by an adult unless the children are very adept with scissors.)

2. Reproduce, color, and cut out the cowboy patterns.

3. Glue the cowboy legs to the front of the container.

4. Apply glue to the empty space below the belt of the cowboy and attach it to the back of the container. Both patterns should be facing in the same direction.

5. Reproduce, color, and design the cowboy card patterns to suit a math or vocabulary topic that needs to be learned and recognized quickly. Cut out the cards.

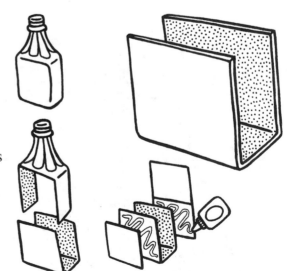

Variations: The card holder can also be used to hold spelling words that students are working on.

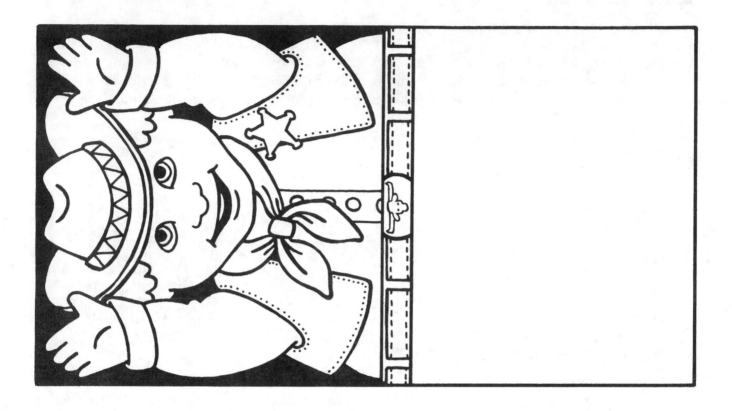

Pigs in the Pen

Links to Literacy

Students can practice counting from 1–10 and skip counting by 2's after making Pigs in the Pen. Instruct students to count each pig as they put it in the Pig Pen. Have students put two pigs in at a time to give them practice skip counting by 2's. To extend the activity, have each student write a number (from 1–10) on each pig pattern. The student can place the pigs in the correct sequence, or count backwards, putting the number 10 pig in first.

Materials

- 16 jumbo craft sticks
- 10 pig patterns (page 131)
- large milk carton
- pink or pale orange copy paper
- brown construction paper
- scissors
- glue
- hot glue gun

Art Project Instructions

1. Cut the milk carton in half and discard the top of the carton, keeping only the open container.

2. Glue brown construction paper over the four sides of the open carton, leaving the hole open.

3. To make the fence posts, arrange four craft sticks on each side (like a # sign) and glue them down.

4. Reproduce the pig pattern page twice onto appropriately colored paper. Cut out the pig patterns.

5. Put the pigs in the Pig Pen.

6. Label the pig pen if appropriate.

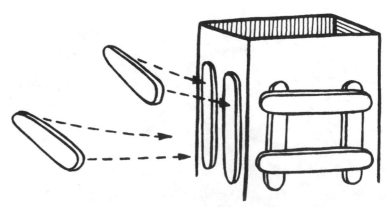

Paper Plate Crayon Container

Links to Literacy

Students can practice counting skills after making the Crayon Container and crayons. Have each student count aloud as he or she places each crayon in the container. To extend the activity, students can demonstrate their knowledge of colors and their ability to read color words. Have students independently color each crayon the correct color by reading and recognizing the word on a corresponding real crayon.

Materials

- 2 large white paper plates
- crayon and container patterns (pages 133–135)
- crayons
- pencils
- scissors
- glue

Art Project Instructions

1. Reproduce and cut out the container patterns.

2. Trace each container pattern onto a separate paper plate as shown and cut the two pieces out.

3. Color the container-front pattern; then glue it onto the traced paper plate piece, so that they fit together.

4. Apply glue around the side and bottom edges of the container-back pattern that was cut out from a paper plate. Glue the front piece to the back.

5. Reproduce, color, and cut out the crayon patterns. (Laminate the crayons for easier use and durability.)

6. Place the crayons in the Paper Plate Crayon Container.

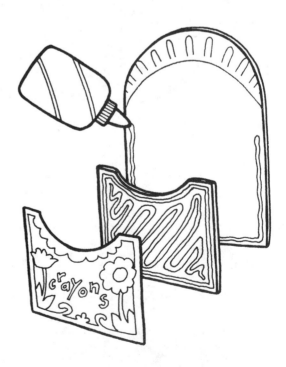

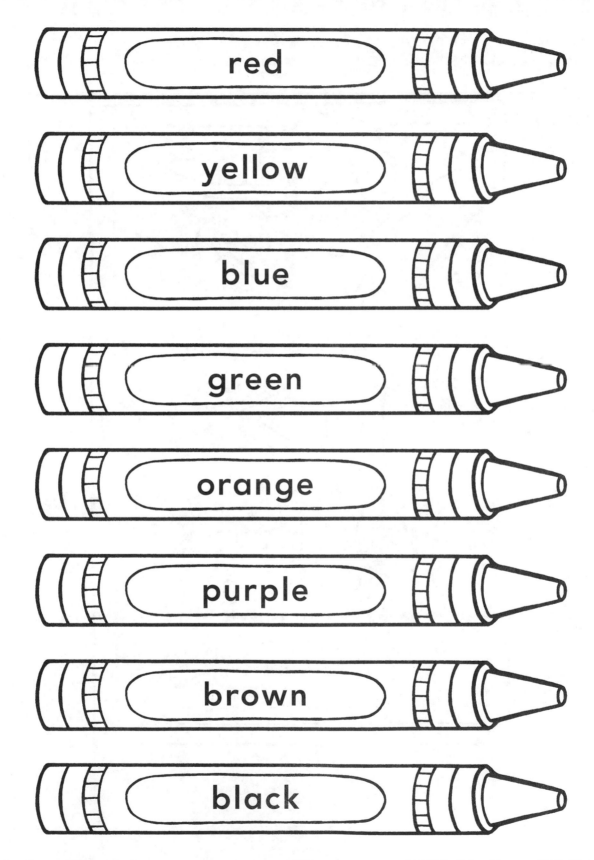

red

yellow

blue

green

orange

purple

brown

black

Dog Bones and House

Links to Literacy

Students can practice counting skills and simple addition and subtraction facts after making the Dog Bones and House. Have each student use the dog bones to create a number path to the doghouse. He or she rolls one or two dice; then counts that number of dog bones from the beginning of the path. The student continues to roll the die or dice and move forward with the little dog marker until reaching the doghouse. The student can play this game alone or with a friend. To extend the activity, write simple addition or subtraction facts on the bones for the student to solve before going on to the next bone.

Materials

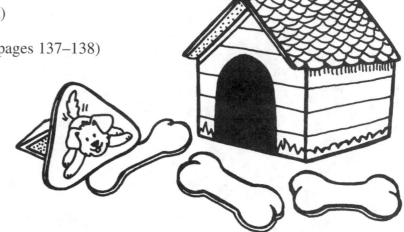

- individual-sized milk carton (½ pint)

- dog, bone, and doghouse patterns (pages 137–138)

- crayons or markers

- scissors

- glue

- dice

Art Project Instructions

1. Glue the opening of the milk carton back to its closed position.

2. Reproduce, color, and cut out the dog, bones, paper strip, and doghouse patterns.

3. Glue the front and back pieces to opposite ends of the carton.

4. Glue the two side pieces onto the sides and top of the carton doghouse.

5. Line up the bones in front of the doghouse to form a path.

6. Fold the paper strip on its three dotted lines. Glue the ends of the strip together to hold it in a triangle shape.

7. Glue one side of the triangle to the back of the dog so the dog stands up.

front

sides

back

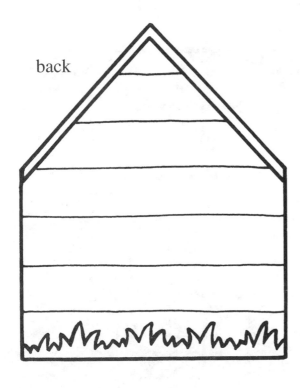

Dog and Bone Patterns

Dog, Bones, and Paper Strip

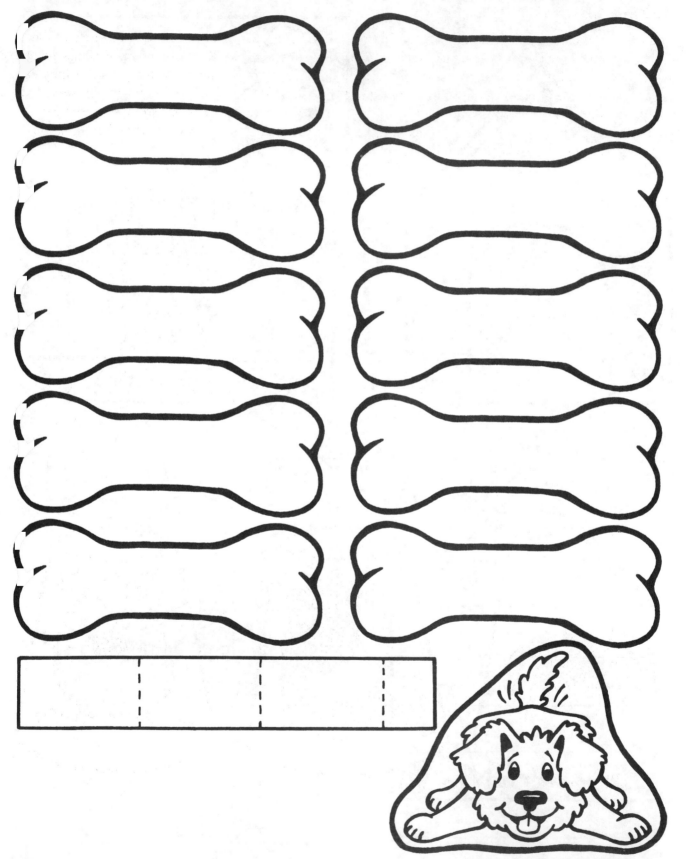

Links to Literacy

Students can practice explaining their feelings while making the Tower of Fears. Read a story to the students that deals with common fears, such as *Bedtime for Frances* by Russell Hoban. Discuss what each child is afraid of. Students can explain each picture they draw on their tower cups and if they can, why they are afraid of that certain thing. Pose questions such as: What do you do when you see something you are afraid of? What fears are of imaginary things and what fears are of real things? What can you do to be less fearful? To extend the activity, number the fears on a scale from what is most frightening to the least frightening.

Materials

- small Styrofoam cups

- markers

Art Project Instructions

1. On each upside-down cup, use markers to draw a picture of a different fear.

2. Color each of the cup pictures.

3. Stack the cups to build the Tower of Fears.

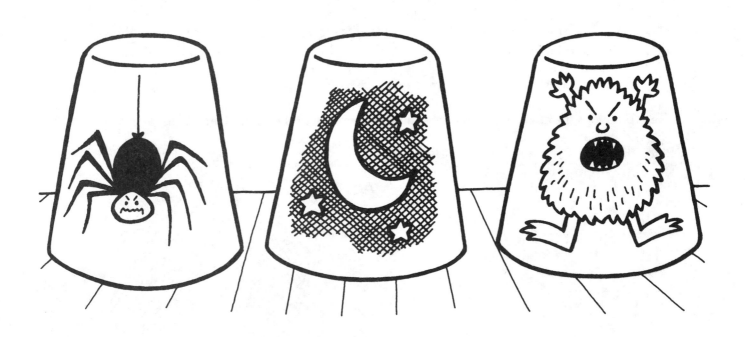

Stick People and Feelings Container

Links to Literacy

Students can develop an understanding of feelings and moods and what causes them before making the Stick People. Discuss different moods and feelings—what they are and what causes them. Each student should look in an individual mirror to make different facial expressions for different moods. Relate colors and expressions to feelings. For example, baby blue could mean *sad* and dark red could mean *angry*. To extend the activity, gain students' attention by placing the Stick People in Feelings Containers. Place all of the Stick People in the happy container; then transfer them into another container when students need to be signalled that they are being too loud. The goal is to keep the sticks in the first container (covered with happy faces).

Materials

- 4 jumbo craft sticks

- small cans or cups

- yellow construction paper

- markers or felt pens

- scissors

- glue

Art Project Instructions

1. Each student designs a set of 4 Stick People (for example, happy, sad, angry, and scared).

2. Use markers to draw a face on the stick; then color the bottom in a color related to the feeling portrayed on the facial expression.

3. Cut out yellow construction paper circles and draw happy faces on them.

4. Glue the happy faces to one of the containers. Leave the other container blank.

5. Place the Stick People in the Happy Face Pail.

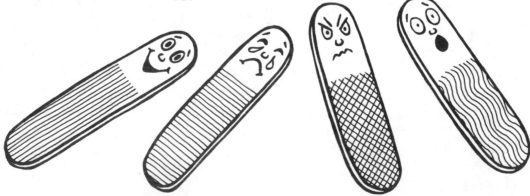

Links to Literacy

Students can practice describing how they feel in different situations. Use the four hats (happy, sad, angry, and scared) to give students an opportunity to discuss their feelings. Tell stories about exciting events, such as going to a friend's house for a party or getting a new bike. Have students hold up their happy hats to show how they would feel if that happened to them. Issues such as bullying or teasing can be discussed, and each student can choose which hat fits for each situation. To extend the activity, have students share real scenarios or role play different times they have been *scared, sad, angry,* or *happy*.

Materials

- 4 white paper bowls

- 4 large white paper plates

- acrylic paints in a variety of colors

- paintbrushes

- markers

- pencil

- scissors

- stapler

Art Project Instructions

1. Place one paper bowl on the center of a paper plate and trace a hat rim. Cut the center circle out of the plate. Cut the center circle slightly smaller than the drawn circle. Place this rim (facedown) over the bowl so it fits around it. Staple the rim to the bowl. Repeat for the remaining bowls and plates.

2. Paint one hat red, another blue hat, one hat in many bright colors, and the last hat orange and green.

3. Label the rims of the hats with a marker. Label the red hat "Angry," the blue hat "Sad," the multicolored hat "Happy," and the last hat "Scared."

Turkey Talk

Links to Literacy

Students can learn how to express their feelings about situations that happen to them. This activity is particularly helpful for students who are not always comfortable opening up about what they are thinking or feeling inside. Use the turkey to get each student to pluck the feeling feather that he or she is experiencing at that moment. A child who is happy and content can take that feather from the turkey to show that he or she is feeling that way. Discussion can be initiated by looking at the feather each child has removed. If a child is upset or scared, you can find out what he or she is feeling. A conference with him or her may help clarify why that child is feeling a certain way.

Materials

- 5 clothespins
- large white paper plate
- turkey patterns (pages 143–144)
- crayons or markers
- scissors
- glue

Art Project Instructions

1. Color the paper plate brown.

2. Reproduce, color, and cut out the turkey patterns.

3. Glue the turkey heads (not the tabs) together.

4. Glue the base of the neck to the middle of the plate, so the head is sticking out.

5. Color the feathers for the turkey. On each feather, draw a picture that depicts a certain feeling. For example, you can draw a picture of playing a fun game with friends on the happy feather. Feathers can represent *happy*, *sad*, *angry*, *bored*, and *scared*. (**Alternative:** Cut out the Feeling Markers at the bottom of the page. Use one for each colored feather. Glue the five completed feathers onto a clothespin.)

6. To attach the feathers to the turkey, glue them to clothespins. Attach the clothespin feathers, side-by-side to the top of the plate.

7. Glue the turkey feet to the bottom of the plate.

Feeling Markers

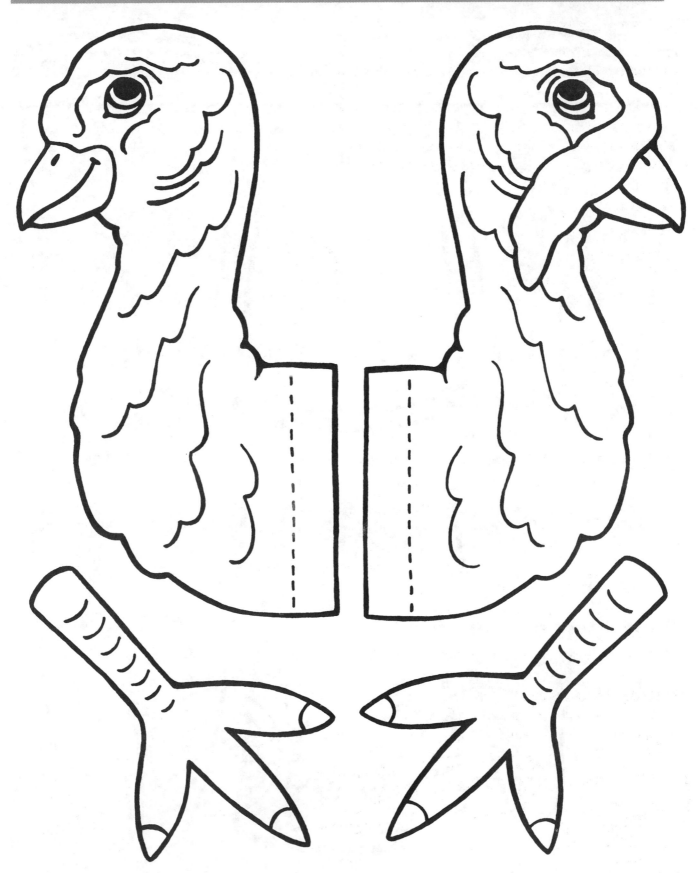

Links to Literacy

Students can practice determining feelings that nursery rhyme characters experience after making the House of Feelings. After the House of Feelings has been created, read nursery rhymes and have students place each character/set of characters in the room that suits the feeling of that particular rhyme. For example, Little Bo Beep can be placed in the worried room, the girls Georgie Porgie kissed can be placed in the sad room, Old King Cole will be placed in the happy room, and Diddle Diddle Dumpling's parents might be put in the angry room. To extend the activity, have students choose one or two nursery rhymes on their own to analyze.

Materials

- shoebox or small box with a lid (per student)

- 4 different colors of acrylic paints and paintbrushes

- scissors

- crayons or markers

- tape or glue

- pattern pieces (pages 146–147)

- book of nursery rhymes (optional)

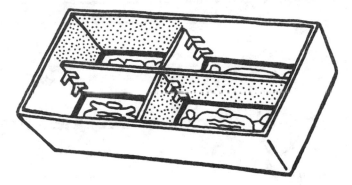

Art Project Instructions

1. Cut the lid of the box to make room dividers for the shoebox. The shoebox should be divided into at least 4 spaces to represent the feelings *sad, scared, happy,* and *angry.*

2. Tape or glue the cut pieces into the shoebox to divide it into rooms.

3. Paint each room a color that is indicative of the feeling it represents. For example, the sad room might be painted blue, and the angry room could be a dark red.

4. Reproduce, color, and cut out the nursery rhyme character patterns.

5. Read different nursery rhymes, such as "Little Bo Peep," "Georgie Porgie," "Old King Cole," "Diddle Diddle Dumpling," and "Little Miss Muffet."

6. Glue the characters in the room that is appropriate for them.

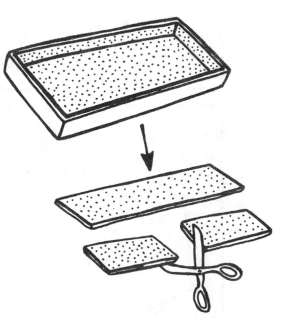

Nursery Rhyme Character Patterns

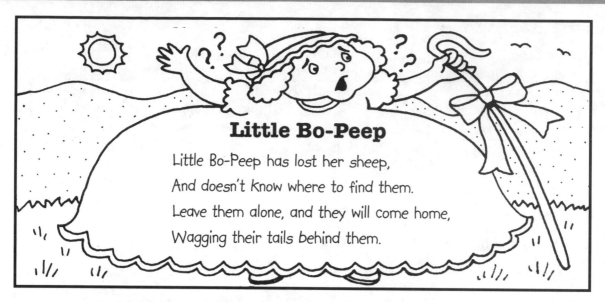

Little Bo-Peep

Little Bo-Peep has lost her sheep,
And doesn't know where to find them.
Leave them alone, and they will come home,
Wagging their tails behind them.

Georgie Porgie

Georgie Porgie
Pudding and pie,
Kissed the girls
and made them cry.

Little Miss Muffet

Little Miss Muffet
Sat on a tuffet,
Eating her curds and whey;
Along came a spider,
Who sat down beside her,
And frigntened Miss Muffet away.

Diddle, Diddle, Dumpling

Diddle, Diddle, Dumpling
My son John,
Went to bed with his trousers on,
One shoe off, the other shoe on,
Diddle, Diddle, Dumpling,
My son John.

Old King Cole

Old King Cole was a merry old soul,
And a merry old soul was he.
He called for his pipe,
And he called for his bowl,
And he called for his fiddlers three.

Paper Plate Poem Picture

Objective: Storytelling

Links to Literacy

Students can record original ideas and read back what they have written after creating the Paper Plate Poem Picture. Students can choose their own topics to write about or a topic can be suggested. Depending on the level of the child, he or she may write words the way they sound, as long as the student is able to read the poem back to you. To extend the activity, have students write poems that follow a word pattern. Or have students begin to grasp the writing process by first writing a rough draft on paper; then transferring a corrected version onto the paper plate.

Materials

- large white paper plate
- writing paper
- crayons or markers
- pencil
- ribbon
- glue

Art Project Instructions

1. On a sheet of writing paper, write a poem about a topic.

2. Use a pencil to lightly draw a picture, in the center of the paper plate, about your poem.

3. Use crayons or markers to print your poem around the picture.

4. Color the picture.

5. Glue ribbon around the edge of the plate to create a pretty frame for your Poem Picture.

Objective: Storytelling

Links to Literacy

Students can use their imagination to tell new and interesting stories while playing with the Story Cubes. Students can roll each cube like a die; then use the pictures on the two cubes to tell a story about the selected character and setting. To extend the activity, students can write out their stories and illustrate them.

Materials

- 2 cube-shaped tissue boxes
- story cube patterns (pages 150–152)
- construction paper
- crayons or markers
- tape
- scissors
- pencil (optional)

Art Project Instructions

1. Using tape, cover the tissue boxes with construction paper.

2. Reproduce, color, and cut out the setting and character story cube patterns. (Or, give students a copy of the blank cube patterns and have them draw settings and characters on them.)

3. Tape the six completed settings on the sides of one of the cubes to form a die of story settings.

4. Tape the six completed characters on the other cube to form a character die.

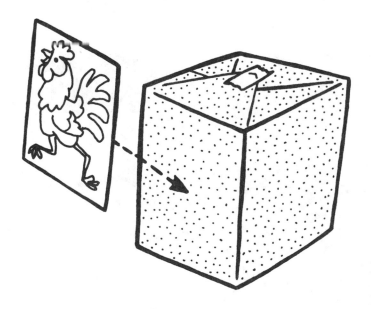

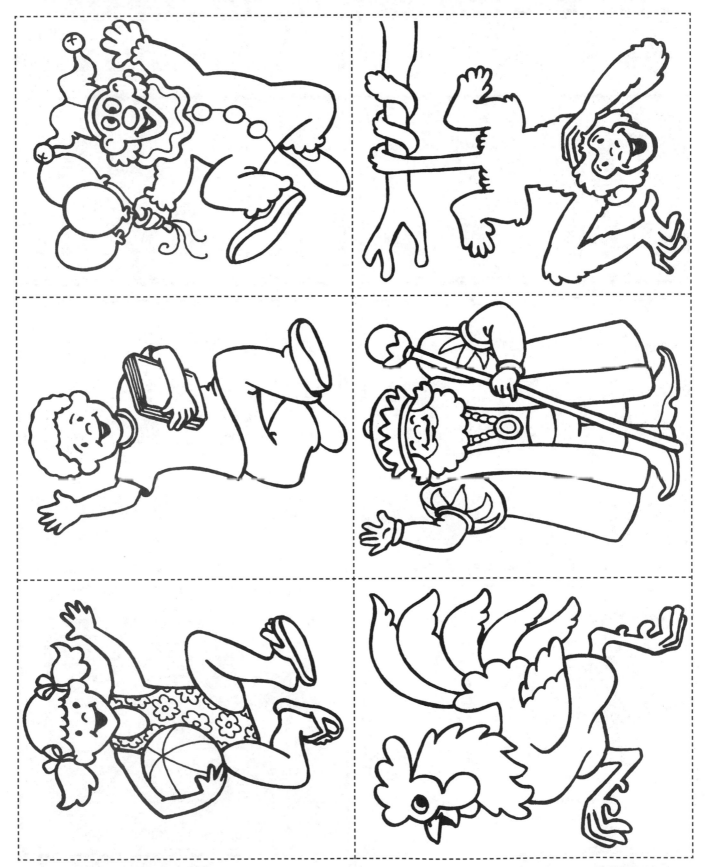

Links to Literacy

Students can use their newly created Crazy Characters to create and tell good guy/bad guy stories. As students twist and turn the robots' arms and legs, new story information can be told. To extend the activity, stories can also focus on real-life situations that students encounter or need to learn about, such as bullying or not talking to strangers.

Materials

- toothpaste box
- 4 mini candy boxes, or raisin boxes
- 4 paper fasteners
- construction paper in a variety of colors
- crayons or markers
- pencil
- glitter glue
- glue
- scissors

Art Project Instructions

1. Using glue, cover all of the boxes in different colors of construction paper, leaving the tops and bottoms of the boxes uncovered.

2. Use a sharpened pencil to carefully poke a hole into one side of each of the four mini boxes. These will create the arms and legs of the Crazy Characters.

3. On both sides of the toothpaste box, use a pencil to poke small holes toward the bottom and above it in the middle. These holes will be used to attach the arms and legs.

4. Insert a paper fastener inside the mini box where a hole has been formed; then push the fastener into one of the holes in the toothpaste box. Close the fastener inside the box. Repeat for the remaining boxes.

5. Use markers and glitter glue to create a different face and body on each side of the box (this will form two different Crazy Characters).

6. Turn the box to the other side to allow the other character to talk.

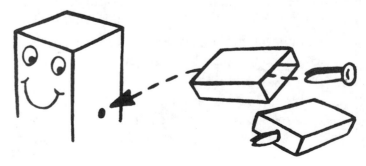

Sturdy Witch

Links to Literacy

Students can create their own Halloween stories using the Sturdy Witch as a prop to manipulate and maneuver. Give students a story starter, such as "One Halloween night, a beautiful witch tried to. . ." Students can complete the story using the prop. To extend the activity, have students write and illustrate their stories.

Materials

- paper lunch bag
- witch patterns (page 155)
- old newspaper
- large tuna or chicken can
- black construction paper
- scissors
- glue
- black and green acrylic paint
- paintbrush
- black ribbon
- curling ribbon (any colors)
- pencil
- crayons or markers
- rubber bands

Art Project Instructions

1. Cut the bottom off the bag and glue the open bag around the outside rim of the can. Secure the bag with a rubber band until dry.

2. Stuff the can with crunched-up newspaper and tie a ribbon around the top of the bag.

3. Paint the top ¾ of the bag black and the bottom ¼ of the bag and the can green.

4. Make hair by adding 1" strips of ribbon and curling it with scissors. Glue the curls to the sides and back of the head.

5. Cut out the hat rim pattern. Remove the gray section. Trace the rim onto black paper. Cut out the rim and slip it over the top of the bag. Glue it in place.

6. Color and cut out the remaining patterns and glue them onto the green part of the bag and can to create the Sturdy Witch. Attach the mouth first, then the nose and the eyes.

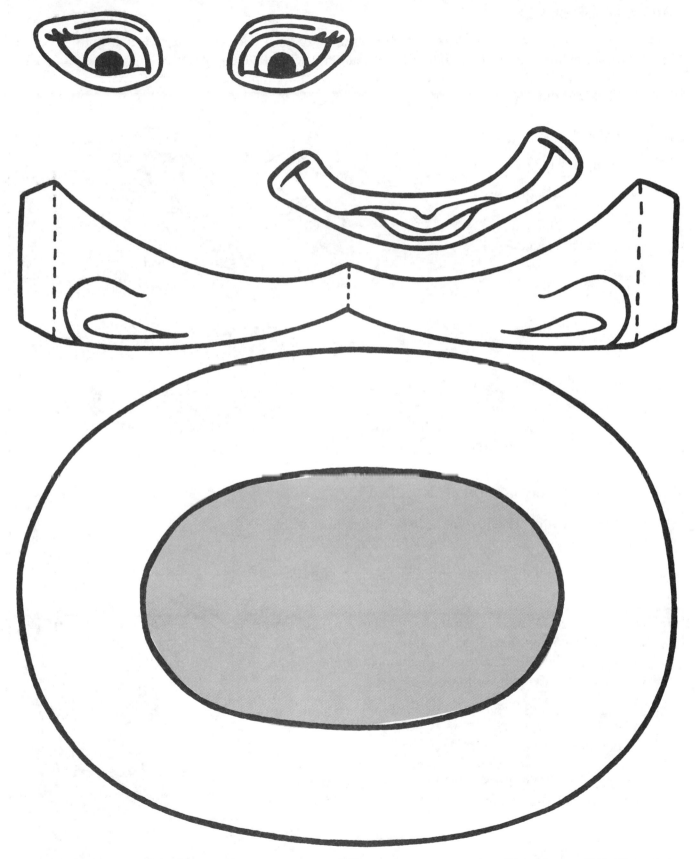

Sturdy Jack o' Lantern

Links to Literacy

Students can create their own Halloween stories using the Sturdy Jack o' Lantern as a prop to manipulate and maneuver. Give students a story starter, such as "One Halloween night, a scary jack o' lantern tried to…" Students can complete the story using the prop. To extend the activity, have students write and illustrate their stories.

Materials

- paper lunch bag
- jack o' lantern patterns (page 157)
- old newspaper
- large tuna or chicken can
- scissors
- glue
- orange and brown acrylic paint
- paintbrush
- green chenille stick
- black and green crayons

Art Project Instructions

1. Cut the bottom off the bag and glue the open bag around the outside rim of the can.

2. Stuff the can with crunched-up newspaper and twist a green chenille stick around the top of the bag to secure it.

3. Paint the can and the bag orange. Paint the top of the bag, above the chenille stick brown. Allow time to dry.

4. Reproduce, color, and cut out the jack o' lantern patterns. Fold the leaf along the dotted lines; then apply glue to Tab A and attach it to the top of the pumpkin under the chenille stick.

5. To make a 3-D nose, fold the nose pattern down along the lines. Apply glue to Tabs B and C. Glue the nose onto the pumpkin's face.

6. Glue the remaining facial features onto the pumpkin.

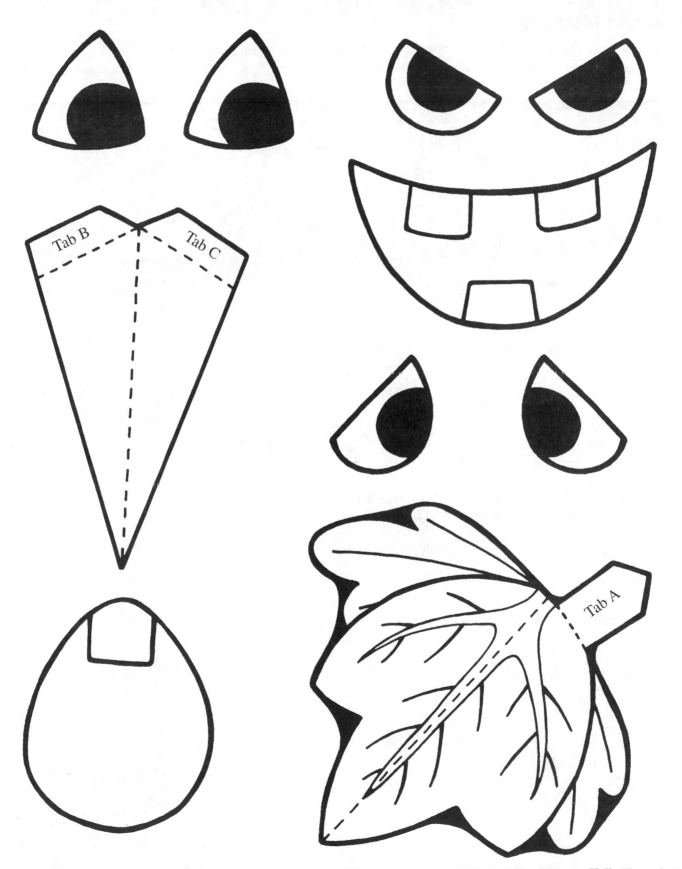

Lazy Leprechaun

Links to Literacy

Students can create, write, and illustrate their own leprechaun stories after making the Lazy Leprechaun. Read a story to the students about a tricky and clever leprechaun, such as *Clever Tom and the Leprechaun* by Linda Shute. Then have students create their own leprechauns from toilet paper tubes. Students can brainstorm what their leprechauns would do if they weren't clever and tricky, but lazy. Make a class story and then have students tell their own leprechaun stories. To extend the activity, have them write out their stories and illustrate them.

Materials

- toilet paper tube

- leprechaun patterns (page 159)

- green acrylic paint or green paper

- paintbrush

- crayons or markers

- scissors

- glue

Art Project Instructions

1. Paint the toilet paper tube green (or cover it with paper) and allow time to dry.

2. Reproduce, color, and cut out the leprechaun patterns.

3. Glue the coat onto the front of the tube.

4. Glue the legs to the inside of the tube so that they stick out in front of the sitting leprechaun.

5. Apply glue atop Tab A. Place the tab on the inside top of the tube.

6. Fold Tabs B and C down and apply glue to them. Attach one arm to each side of the Lazy Leprechaun.

Tab A

Tab B

Tab C

Silly Snowman

Links to Literacy

Students can write creative Silly Snowman stories after creating the paper plate snowman. Discuss with students what you need to make a snowman. Read a story about a snowman that comes to life or sing the song, "Frosty the Snowman." Make up a class story about a snowman and what adventures could happen if the snowman magically came to life. Each student can then draw a picture or write a story of his or her own on the pages attached to the paper plate snowman. To extend the activity, have each student take a turn sharing his or her story with the class.

Materials

- 2 small white paper plates
- snowman patterns (page 161)
- 2 circle story and twig arm patterns (page 162)
- crayons or markers
- scissors
- glue
- stapler
- pencil

Art Project Instructions

1. Reproduce, color, and cut out the snowman patterns.

2. To make the head of the snowman, glue the hat, eyes, and mouth onto one of the paper plates.

3. To make the nose, fold the pattern in half along the dotted line. Fold Tabs A downward. Apply glue atop the tabs and attach the nose to the middle of the paper-plate face.

4. To create the body, staple another plate below the head plate.

5. Make two copies of the story circles and twig arms. Cut them out.

6. Fold the story pages upward along the uppermost dotted line. Attach the pages together by applying glue to the part of the circle above the dotted line.

7. Write a Silly Snowman story on the circle story patterns.

8. Glue the pages to the body plate.

9. Glue one twig arm to each side of the snowman by applying glue to Tabs B. Attach the arms behind the body plate so they stick out on either side.

Tab A

Tab A

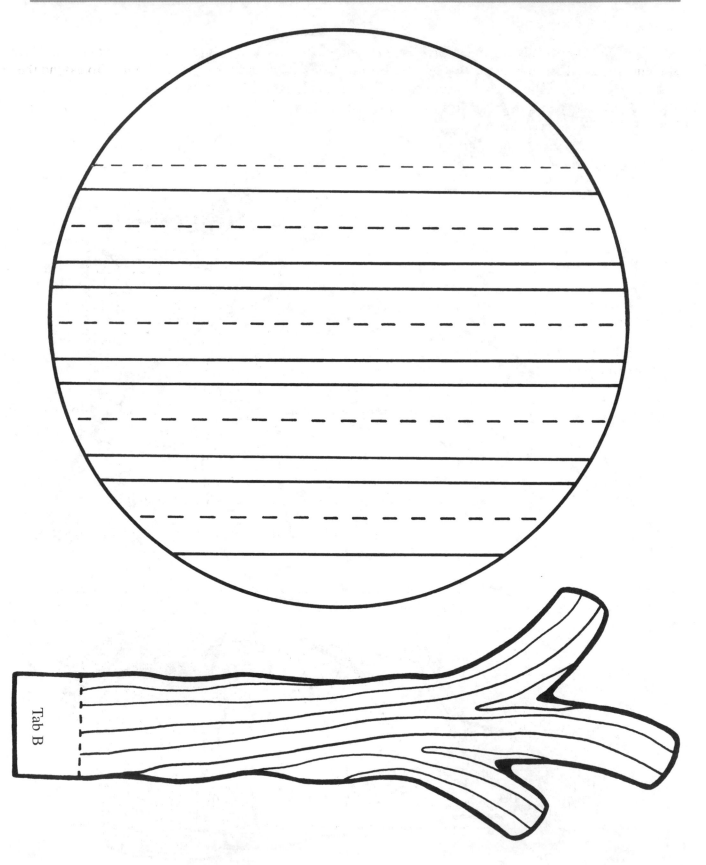

Tab B

Objective: Storytelling

Links to Literacy

Each student can practice writing journal entries and his or her name while making a Journal Jar. Have students focus on finding letters that are needed for their names and the word, *journals*. To extend the activity, have them use letters or pictures to decorate their Journal Jars. When the jars are finished, students can use them to store their favorite journal entries. They can be used as a portfolio for their best work in journal writing.

Materials

- glass or plastic peanut butter jar and lid

- old magazines or stickers

- glue

- scissors

- pencil

- writing paper

Art Project Instructions

1. Peel off any labels from the jar.

2. Use old magazines or stickers to find letters to spell the word, *Journals*, and the student's name. Cut the letters out and glue them onto the container (for example, Dave's Journals).

3. Finish decorating the Journal Jar by gluing pictures or other words cut out from old magazines onto the jar.

4. Write a journal story on writing paper. Have the student share the journal idea with a friend. Later, roll the paper up and place it inside the Journal Jar.

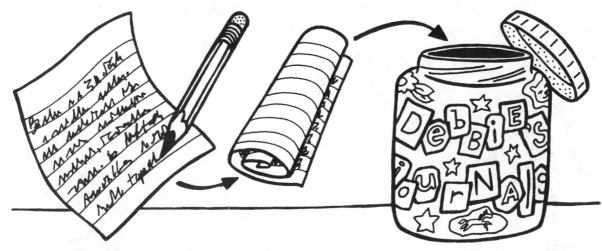

Personalized Skateboard

Links to Literacy

Each student can practice writing his or her name while creating a Personalized Skateboard. Some students have difficulty with printing and spelling their names. In the middle of the oval, have each student print his or her name in big letters. Instruct him or her to outline the letters with another color; then continue to use different colors of markers to outline the letters until the skateboard shape is completely colored. In this way, he or she can continuously see the letters in the name. To extend the activity, have each student write his or her last name or middle name.

Materials

- 2 cotton swabs
- toilet paper tube
- bright-colored markers
- scissors
- tape

Art Project Instructions

1. Cut out a large oval shape from the toilet paper tube, so that the sides have a bit of an upward flare. (**Note:** Longer names may require larger ovals.)

2. To make the wheels for the Personalized Skateboard, cut a cotton swab in half and put the halves together by taping the middle. Repeat with the second cotton swab. Tape these to the bottom of the skateboard with one at the front and one at the back.

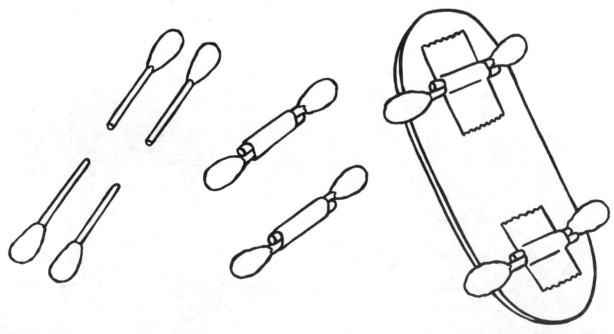

Objective: Word recognition

Links to Literacy

Students can learn to recognize names after creating Shaker Sticks. Go through the names of students in the classroom and have the students write their names out for everyone to see. For each name, have students shake their Shaker Sticks to determine how many beats (or syllables) each name has. Put a slash between the letters for a break in each name (for example: Ka/ty or Cor/y). To extend the activity, use last names as well.

Materials

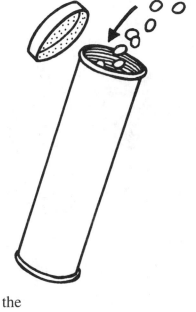

- tall potato chip container and lid

- bright-colored construction paper

- tape and glue

- stickers

- uncooked pasta, beads, or beans

- markers or crayons

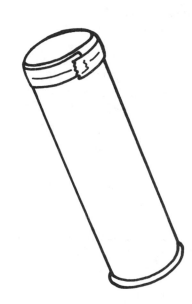

Art Project Instructions

1. Drop a handful of uncooked pasta into the potato chip tube and replace the lid. Tape the lid back on the tube to secure it.

2. Using tape or glue, cover the tube with construction paper.

3. Using markers and stickers, decorate the paper.

Name Blocks

Links to Literacy

Each student can practice recognizing and spelling his or her own name after making the Name Puzzle. Have the student mix up the boxes; then put them together like a puzzle. Or the student can print his or her name decoratively on blank squares; then cut them apart to put the name back together using the puzzle boxes. To extend the activity, have children combine their boxes and see if they can spell their last names or other special words.

Materials

- foam sheets, small boxes, foam core, or blocks

- name puzzle patterns (page 167)

- scissors

- glue

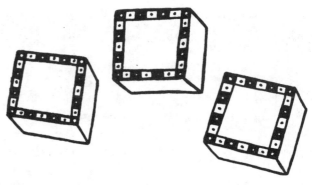

- crayons or markers

Art Project Instructions

1. Reproduce, color, and cut out the name puzzle patterns.

2. Cut the foam sheets into 2" (5 cm) squares.

3. Write a different letter of the student's name on each "block." Glue each block pattern to a different square.

Hansel and Gretel Puppets

Links to Literacy

Students can develop retelling skills using their newly created Hansel and Gretel Puppets. Have them use the puppets as props while they retell the story, "Hansel and Gretel." In summary, two children go into the woods and lose their way. The children come across a candy house and start to eat the candy. A witch that lives in that house tricks Hansel and Gretel and locks them in a cage. Finally, the children escape by tricking the witch and return home to their distraught father. To extend the activity, make a candy house to use in the dramatization.

Materials

- 2 paper lunch bags

- 4 paper fasteners

- Hansel and Gretel patterns (pages 169–170)

- crayons or markers

- scissors

- glue

Art Project Instructions

1. Reproduce, color, and cut out the Hansel and Gretel patterns.

2. Glue the head piece to the bottom of the closed end of the bag and the mouth piece just underneath, so that it appears that each puppet can talk.

3. Attach one arm to each side of the bag by using a paper fastener. Insert the paper fasteners and open them inside the bag.

4. Draw buttons and a collar to create the boy's shirt and the girl's dress top.

5. Glue on the pants for the boy and the skirt for the girl.

6. Insert your hand into each bag to move the Hansel or Gretel Puppet.

168

Gretel Patterns

Links to Literacy

Each student can practice recalling story events after making the Paper Plate Pinocchio. Each student can use his or her clothespin nose (attached to the chenille stick) to make it grow when Pinocchio tells a lie. Then, he or she makes the nose small again at the end of the tale. To extend the activity, talk about the importance of telling the truth.

Materials

- 9 toilet paper tubes
- 4 paper fasteners
- infant-sized outfit with socks and mittens
- small white paper plate
- clothespin
- chenille stick
- packing tape or stapler
- scissors
- pen and markers

Art Project Instructions

1. Use a pen to create a small hole in two toilet paper tubes. Press the paper fastener through 1 tube at a time; then close the fastener inside. Repeat this step twice so that there are 2 legs.

2. Tape three of the other toilet paper tubes together. This will be Pinocchio's body.

3. Connect the legs to the body with packing tape.

4. Use another paper fastener to connect a toilet paper tube to the top roll of the body. Repeat this step twice to create both arms.

5. Draw and color Pinocchio's face and hair on the back of the plate, cutting a small hole in the center for the nose.

6. Tape or staple the chenille stick to the front of the plate at the top and the bottom.

7. Place the clothespin through the center hole in the plate and clip it onto the chenille stick at the back to hold it in place.

8. Tape the head to the top of Pinocchio's body.

9. Dress Pinocchio in an infant outfit with socks and mittens.

Old MacDonald's Farm

Links to Literacy

Students can practice listening and sequencing skills after creating Old MacDonald's Farm. Read, sing, or tell a version of "Old MacDonald's Farm" that has a variety of animals in it. Have students work on sequencing by recalling which animal comes in which order, according to the version just heard. Have students place animals in the barn, in the same sequence as the song, as they name the animals. To extend the activity, evaluate students' listening and sequencing skills using the form on page 175.

Materials

- small cereal box

- farm patterns (pages 173–174)

- soup can

- red and yellow construction paper

- glue

- tape

- scissors

- crayons or markers

Art Project Instructions

1. Cut the top off the cereal box.

2. Cover the entire box with red construction paper using tape or glue.

3. Reproduce, color, and cut out the farm patterns.

4. Glue the barn doors and hayloft to the front of the cereal box.

5. To make a haystack use the yellow paper and the soup can. Cut enough yellow paper to cover the can, leaving a little to go over the edges. Cut small strips along both sides of the paper and fray them to create the look of hay. Glue this around the can to cover it. Gather and tape the strips together at one end of the can. This will form the top of the haystack. Spread the strips at the other end to make the base of the haystack.

6. Glue the Old MacDonald pattern to the barn.

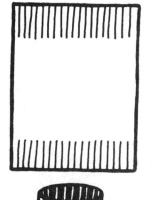

Listening and Sequencing Evaluation Form

If the animal is placed in the correct order, write yes; if the animal is placed incorrectly, write no.

Student's Name	Animal #1	Animal #2	Animal #3	Animal #4

Mermaid

Links to Literacy

Students can practice recalling specific story events after creating the Mermaid Person. Read the fairy tale, "The Little Mermaid." By flipping the mermaid tail behind the body, each student can change the mermaid into a person when she makes the deal with the sea witch. To extend the activity, create a sea witch that transforms into a person.

Materials

- 2 sheets of white cardstock

- mermaid patterns (page 177)

- paper fastener

- glue

- construction paper

- crayons or markers

- scissors

- yarn

- pencil

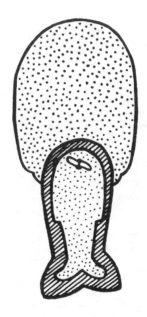

Art Project Instructions

1. Reproduce the mermaid patterns onto white cardstock; then cut out the patterns.

2. Decorate the head, body, and legs with construction paper and crayons or markers. Glue yarn on top of the head for hair.

3. Use a sharpened pencil to carefully poke a hole (as marked) into the bottom middle of the body, the top of the legs, and the mermaid tail.

4. Insert a paper fastener into the hole in the body, then into the mermaid tail, and finally into the legs. Loosely close the fastener to secure it so that the mermaid tail can swing up and hide behind the head, leaving the legs showing.

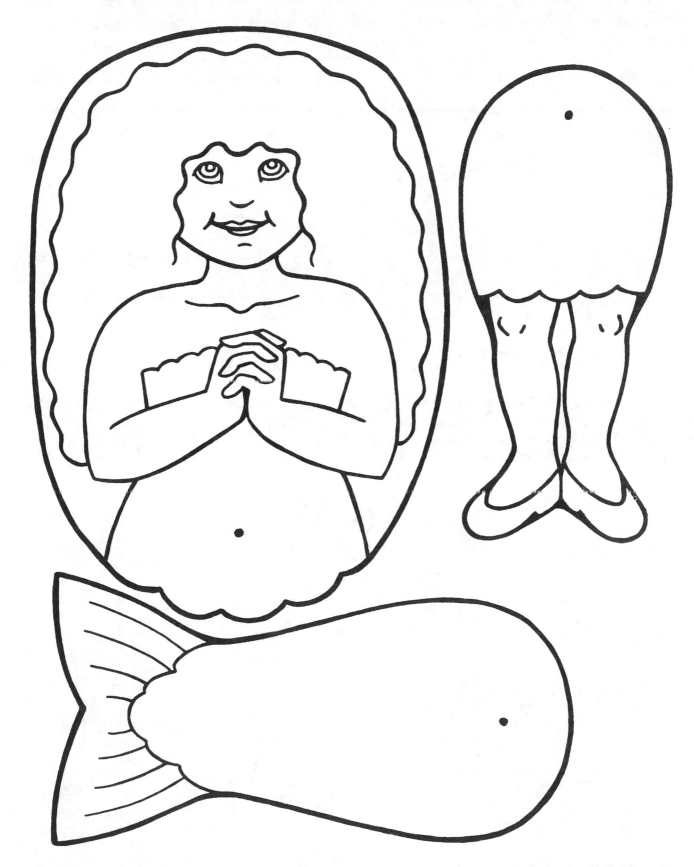

The Importance of Fine and Gross Motor Coordination

A large component of literacy is the ability to print on paper to convey meaning. For students to be able to express their ideas in print formation and then handwriting, they must first develop their hand-eye coordination and fine and gross motor coordination. It is often difficult for many children to print and write legibly when they first begin the process of forming letters on paper with a pencil. Have students practice their coordination by following along dotted lines, drawing circular shapes, or staying between two pathways with their pencils.

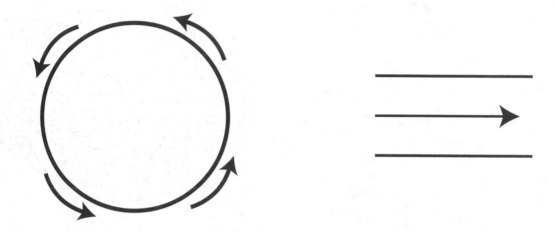

Art projects can also be used to develop finger and hand-eye coordination. In the upcoming section of art ideas and projects, the focus of each activity is fine and gross motor coordination. Using scissors to cut out project pieces, tracing patterns or shapes, gluing small pieces together, and weaving and folding are all ways that students need to use their hands and fingers to maneuver small objects and build coordination.

Links to Literacy

Students can practice letter identification skills by collecting items, which begin with a certain letter, to place in the Basket. To extend the activity, have students place items of a certain color or size in the Basket.

Materials

- small plastic fruit basket

- yarn in a variety of colors

- chenille stick

- scissors

- ruler

- tape

Art Project Instructions

1. Cut the yarn into lengths of about 2' (61 cm). Wrap tape around one end of the yarn. The tape will make going in and out of the holes easier. Tie the untaped end of the yarn to the basket.

2. Start at a bottom side of the fruit basket. Weave one strand of yarn in and out of the plastic squares until you have gone all the way around the sides to the place where you started. Tie the yarn together in a knot so that it does not come loose. Cut off any extra yarn after the knot is tied.

3. Using a different color of yarn, start just above the first yarn. Again weave in and out of the plastic squares until you have gone all the way around the basket. Tie the ends together in a secure knot. Cut off any extra yarn.

4. Repeat step 3, alternating the yarn colors in the weaving, until you have reached the top of the basket. (**Note:** This activity is time consuming. If possible, break up the time into two or three sessions.)

5. To make a basket handle, attach a chenille stick to the top of the basket by pushing one end of the stick through the top middle square of the basket and twisting it in place. Attach the other end of the stick to the opposite side of the basket and twist it securely in place.

Fire and Logs

Links to Literacy

Students can practice storytelling skills after making the Fire and Logs. Pile fake logs in a circular arrangement to create a pretend campfire. Have students share their favorite stories around the campfire. To extend the activity, have students share what they might see, hear, touch, or taste on a camping trip.

Materials

- paper towel tubes

- toilet paper tubes

- other cardboard cylinders

- orange and red tissue paper

- orange and red cellophane

- scissors

- glue

- brown tempera paint or brown paper

- paintbrush

Art Project Instructions

1. Paint the cardboard tubes brown (or cover them with paper) and allow time to dry. These will be the logs for the fire.

2. Cut the cellophane and tear the tissue paper. Pieces can be approximately 6" to 8" square (15 cm to 20 cm).

3. In the middle of the tubes, carefully cut a line that does not extend to each end. Stuff some of the tissue-paper "flames" through the slits in the tubes so that the ends of the flames appear to be shooting out from the log.

4. Arrange the logs in a circular fashion. Larger logs should be on the bottom. You can glue them together to keep them in a pile.

5. Stuff extra "flames" between logs.

Objective: Motor coordination

Links to Literacy

Students can build phonics and sequencing skills after making Egg Cup Trucks. Label both sides of each truck with a letter (from a–z). Have students line up the trucks in alphabetical order. To extend the activity, allow students to form words using the letters on the trucks.

Materials

- Styrofoam egg cup
- small match box or thumbtack box
- construction paper
- glue
- tape
- scissors
- felt pen

Art Project Instructions

1. Cover the small box with construction paper using tape, leaving the ends open so that the inside box can still be pushed in and out.

2. Apply a small amount of glue around the egg-cup rim; then glue it to the front top of the box.

3. Cut out four small construction-paper wheels and glue two wheels to each side of the box.

4. Use the felt pen to draw windows and doors on the cab of the Egg Cup Truck.

5. Pull the inside box out to form the truck bed.

Paper Dolls

Links to Literacy

Students can practice retelling stories, songs, or poems after making paper dolls. Have students retell the poem, "Jack and Jill" using the paper dolls as props. To extend the activity, have students create stories of their own based on the paper dolls.

Materials

- toilet paper tubes

- paper doll patterns (pages 183–184)

- pencil

- paints or markers

- paintbrush

- scissors

- removable sticky adhesive

Art Project Instructions

1. Reproduce and cut out the paper doll patterns.

2. Using removable sticky adhesive, attach each doll pattern around a tube and trace it with a pencil.

3. Carefully cut around the traced lines on the tubes. Be careful not to cut off the base.

4. Decorate the boy, the girl, and the clothes with paints or markers.

5. Dress the boy and the girl with the clothes by bending the tabs backward to keep the clothes on.

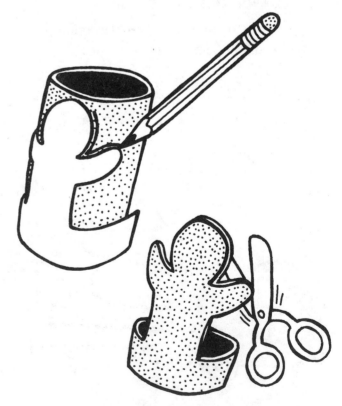

Christmas Tree Mobile

Links to Literacy

Each student can practice writing his or her name while creating the Christmas Tree Mobile. Have each student print his or her name on the gift tags to pretend he or she is giving the gifts to friends or family. To extend the activity, have students brainstorm types of gifts they would like to give.

Materials

- large white paper plate
- mobile patterns (page 186)
- dark green acrylic paint
- paintbrush
- silver or gold glitter glue
- construction paper
- crayons or markers
- scissors
- glue
- string
- hole punch
- ruler

Art Project Instructions

1. Paint the tree green and allow time to dry.

2. Fold the paper plate in half. Fold the plate in half again so it forms a quarter of the plate size.

3. Starting at the tip of the folded plate, cut curved lines on alternating sides, about ½" (1.3 cm) apart. Stop cutting each line at least ½" (1.3 cm) before you reach the edge.

4. Unfold carefully and stretch the plate into a tree shape.

5. Decorate the tree with silver or gold glitter glue to make tinsel and garland.

6. To make decorations, cut out small construction-paper circles of different colors and glue them onto the tree.

7. Reproduce, color, and cut out the mobile patterns.

8. Punch holes in the patterns where marked.

9. Punch four holes into the bottom of the tree. Using string, hang the gifts at different levels from the created holes.

10. Thread a piece of string through the hole in the star. Glue the star to the top of the tree. Form a loop and tie a knot in the string so that the tree can be displayed.

Mobile Patterns

Reindeer Container

Objective: Motor coordination

Links to Literacy

Students can practice counting and skip counting skills after making the Reindeer Container. Give each student 20 dry beans. Have him or her drop the beans into the Reindeer Container while counting each one. Or, have the student drop the beans into the container by 2's, 4's, or 5's. To extend the activity, instruct students to place small pictures of things in the container that a real reindeer would eat.

Materials

- 2 small paper drinking cups
- 4 mini craft sticks
- toilet paper tube
- reindeer patterns (page 188)
- brown acrylic paint
- paintbrush
- crayons or markers
- scissors
- glue gun
- glue

Art Project Instructions

1. Carefully cut a rectangular section out of the sides of the toilet paper tube.

2. Glue one paper cup onto each end of the tube to close off the ends.

3. Paint the tube, craft sticks, and the paper cups brown. Allow time to dry.

4. To make the reindeer legs, use a glue gun to attach one craft stick to each side of both cups.

5. Reproduce, color, and cut out the reindeer patterns.

6. Fold Tabs A upward. Glue the two heads together with the printed sides showing. Apply glue under Tabs A and attach the head to one end of the closed-off tube.

7. To make the tail, fold Tabs B upward; then glue the tails together with the printed sides showing. Apply glue under the tabs and attach the tail to the other end of the tube.

8. Cut the dashed lines on the reindeer's head and antlers. Slide the antlers and ears onto the head.

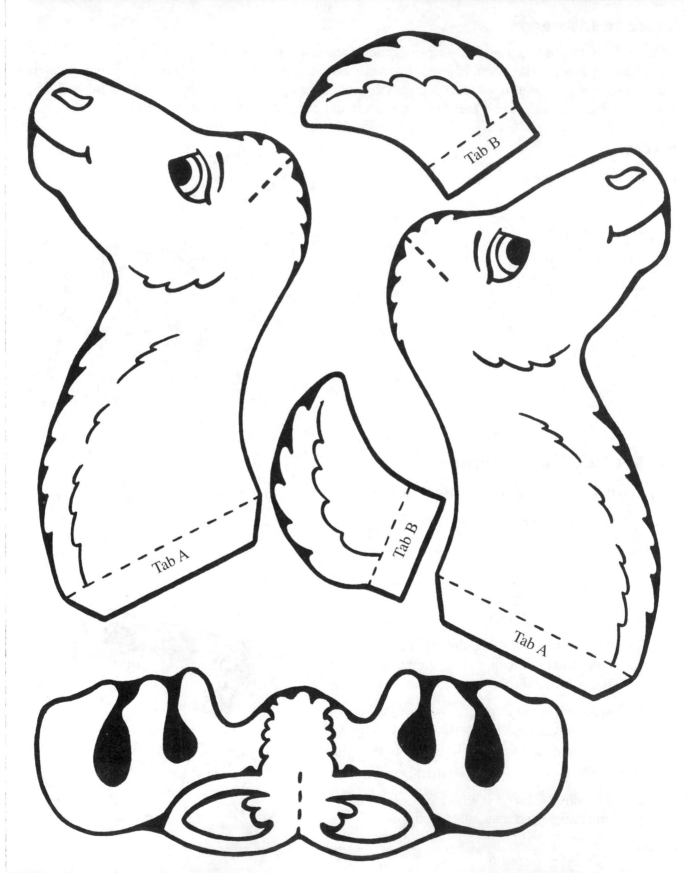

Links to Literacy

Students can practice beginning sound and classification skills after making the Paper Plate Apatosaurus. Have students cut out small pictures, which begin with the letter Aa, from old magazines. Have them glue each cutout on a separate plate of the Apatosaurus. To extend the activity, have students locate cutouts of food that this dinosaur might eat. Explain that we think the Apatosaurus was an herbivore. Then have them glue the cutouts on the body section of the Apatosaurus.

Materials

- 6 large white paper plates
- 14 small white paper plates
- Apatosaurus pattern (page 190)
- green acrylic paint or green paper
- paintbrush
- green crayon or marker
- glue
- scissors
- stapler

Art Project Instructions

1. Paint all of the small paper plates and five of the large paper plates green (or cover them with paper) and allow time to dry.

2. Cut the rim off one small plate.

3. To make the neck of the Apatosaurus, use four small plates, placed side-by-side, and staple the edges together.

4. Reproduce, color, and cut out the Apatosaurus head pattern. Glue the completed head atop the center of the unpainted plate; then cut off the remainder of the plate. Staple the head to the neck of the Apatosaurus.

5. To make the body, use five large plates. Staple them together (as shown); then staple the neck to the opening at the top of the body.

6. Make the tail by stapling five small plates together; then staple the small, cut plate to the end.

7. To make each leg, staple two small plates to the bottom of the body (as shown).

8. Before moving the Paper Plate Apatosaurus, fill in the spots around the staples with glue and allow time to dry.

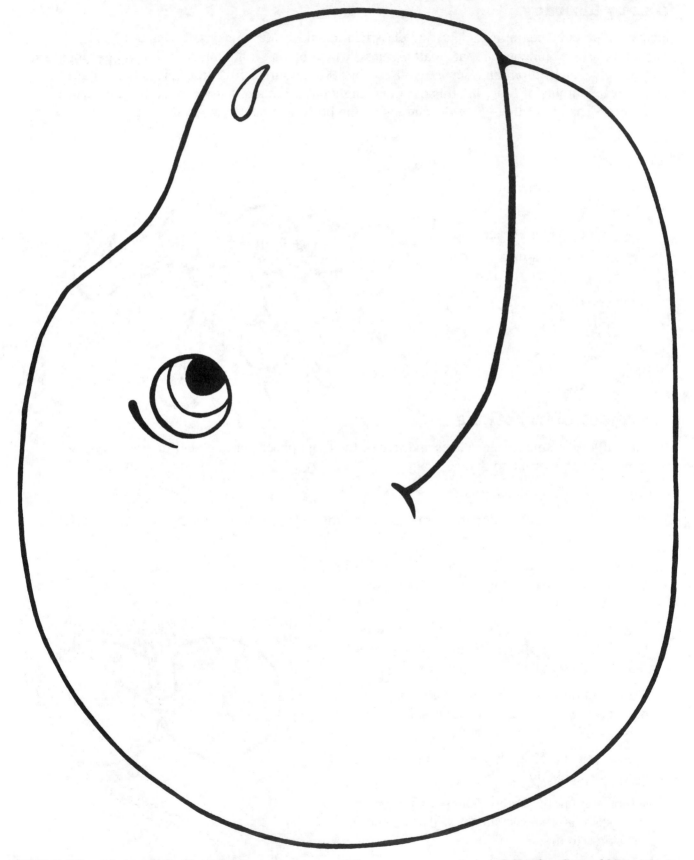

Links to Literacy

Students can practice storytelling skills after creating the Lion Head. Have each student pretend he or she is a lion, and tell about a day the lion has had. Encourage the student to draw pictures and use the Lion Head while telling the lion story. To extend the activity, have students display their Lion Heads during the month of March on a bulletin board titled, "In Like a Lion…"

Materials

- 2 Styrofoam egg cups
- large white paper plate
- lion pattern (page 192)
- brown powder tempera paint
- yellow acrylic paint
- paintbrush
- quilt batting
- scissors
- glue

Art Project Instructions

1. Paint the two egg cups yellow and allow time to dry.

2. Sprinkle the brown powder tempera paint onto the quilt batting until it is fully covered.

3. Allow time for the paint to set and then shake any excess powder off into the garbage. (The powder needs 20-30 seconds to settle into the batting.)

4. Reproduce the lion pattern. Paint the paper plate and the pattern yellow and allow time to dry. Cut out the lion pattern.

5. Glue the lion pattern atop the plate.

6. Glue the batting around the plate, making sure not to cover the face.

7. To make the lion ears, glue one egg cup on each side of the top of the Lion Head. Apply glue around the egg-cup rims and press firmly onto the batting.

Lion Pattern

Lion Head

Links to Literacy

Students can build creative thinking skills after making the Astronaut. Encourage students to imagine what it would be like to walk on the moon. Allow time for several students to share their ideas. To extend the activity, have students dramatize astronauts walking on the moon by manipulating their Astronauts in a sandbox.

Materials

- 2 empty pudding cups
- paper lunch bag
- astronaut patterns (pages 194–195)
- aluminum foil
- old newspaper
- gray acrylic paint
- paintbrush
- crayons or markers
- scissors
- glue
- tape

Art Project Instructions

1. Stuff the paper bag half full with crunched up newspaper; then, fold the top of the bag down and glue it closed.

2. Paint the two pudding cups with gray paint and allow time to dry. Place glue around the top rim of the pudding cups and glue them to the bottom of the paper bag to make the legs of the astronaut.

3. Reproduce, color, and cut out the astronaut patterns.

4. Glue the front and back of the astronaut to the front and back of the bag. Tape the tops of the two heads together.

5. Tape pieces of aluminum foil to the two sides of the bag that are exposed.

6. Fold Tabs A downward and apply glue to them; then attach the front arms to the sides of the bag. Fold Tabs B downward and apply glue to them; then attach the back arms to the sides of the bag.

7. Tape the hands together on each side, as shown.

Tab A

Tab A

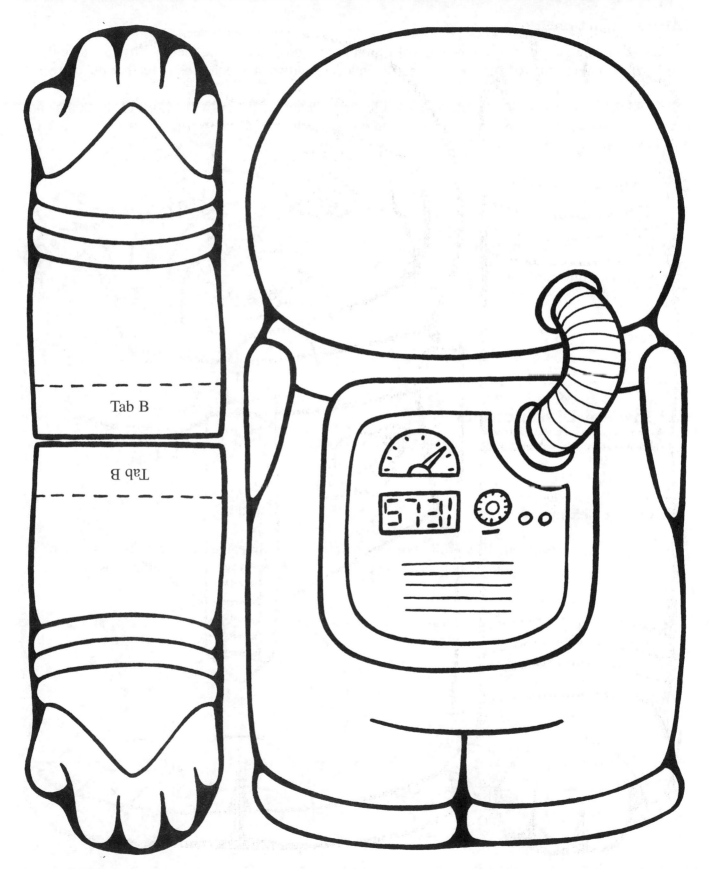

Tab B

Tab B

Rooster

Links to Literacy

Students can demonstrate their knowledge of beginning sounds, colors, and their ability to read color words while making the Rooster. Have students independently color each rooster feather the correct color by reading and recognizing the word on a corresponding crayon. To extend the activity, write a simple addition or subtraction problem on each feather; then write the answer on one of the bumps on the rooster's back. A student solves the problem on the feather; then uses a paper fastener to attach it to the corresponding answer.

Materials

- 5 paper fasteners
- rooster patterns (page 197)
- sheet of white cardstock
- pencil
- crayons
- scissors

Art Project Instructions

1. Reproduce the rooster patterns onto white cardstock.

2. Color each feather if appropriate; then color the rooster's body.

3. Cut out the patterns.

4. Using a sharpened pencil, carefully poke a small hole in each feather (as marked). Using a paper fastener, attach each colored feather to the corresponding beginning letter on the rooster's body.

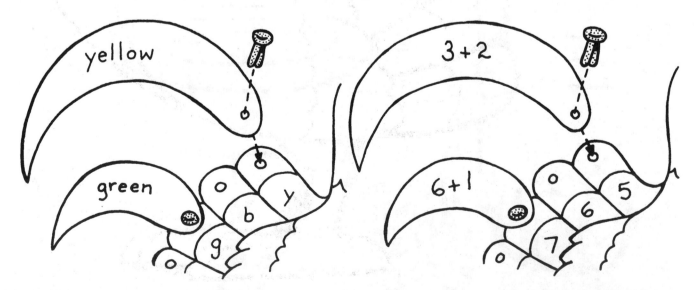

yellow

brown

green

pink

red

Fan Napkin Ring

Links to Literacy

Students can learn more about the Japanese culture before making the Fan Napkin Ring. Share a story that includes the special art of origami, such as *Yoko's Paper Cranes* by Rosemary Wells. Then have students complete the Fan Napkin Ring. To extend the activity, have students try other folding activities to attach to additional napkin rings.

Materials

- toilet paper tube

- wrapping paper or construction paper

- ribbon

- hot glue gun and glue

- scissors

- small plastic flowers (optional)

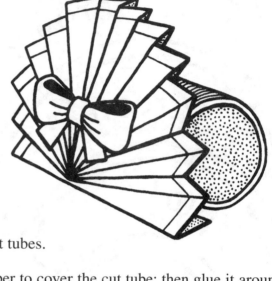

Art Project Instructions

1. Cut the toilet paper tube into thirds. Set aside two cut tubes.

2. Cut out a piece of wrapping paper or construction paper to cover the cut tube; then glue it around the tube.

3. Around both sides of the tube napkin ring, glue ribbon along the inside edge.

4. Cut a 4" x 6" (10 x 15 cm) rectangle from the same paper to make a fan.

5. Do an accordion-style fold with the rectangle by making a fold about ½" (1.3 cm); then flipping it over and making another ½" (1.3 cm) fold and so on, until you get to the end. Take the folded paper and fold it in half; then apply glue along the center to hold the fan together. Press it together so that it stays; then carefully open up the fan.

6. Along the inside edges of the fan, glue ribbon to decorate it. In the middle front of the small fan, glue a bow or small plastic flowers.

7. Glue the back of the fan to the napkin ring.

Links to Literacy

Students can build word recognition skills after making the Simple Gift Bag. On small pieces of paper, write the numbers (from 1–10); then write the corresponding number words (one–ten) on other pieces of paper. Have students draw two papers at a time, and try to match each number to its number word. To extend the activity, have each student write a short poem to the recipient of the bag; then attach it to the bag. As student's word recognition skills increase, add new words and symbols. Try shape words, spelling lists, or other sight words.

Materials

- paper lunch bag
- wrapping paper
- pencil
- glue
- hole punch
- ribbon
- scissors

Art Project Instructions

1. Open the paper bag and lay it down on the wrapping paper.

2. Using a pencil, trace each side of the bag onto the paper.

3. Cut out the traced patterns.

4. Glue each piece onto the correct side of the bag, so that the bag is completely covered.

5. Fold the top of the bag downward, about 1" (2.5 cm). Use a hole punch to put two holes, through all layers, in the center of the fold.

6. Feed the ribbon through the holes and tie a bow in the front to complete the Simple Gift Bag.

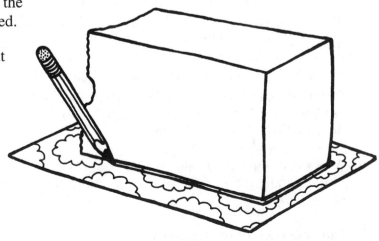

Happy Hippo Helper

Links to Literacy

Students can practice storytelling and beginning sound skills before making the Happy Hippo Helper. Share with students a *George and Martha* book by James Marshall. Have students use the Happy Hippo Helper as a puppet to retell their favorites parts of the story. To extend the activity, have students cut out pictures from magazines, which begin with the letter **Hh**, and put them in the Happy Hippo Helper mouth.

Materials

- 2 egg carton cups (white)
- large white paper plate
- shoe box
- gray acrylic paint
- paintbrush
- gray, black, and white construction paper
- scissors
- glue
- tape
- crayons or markers

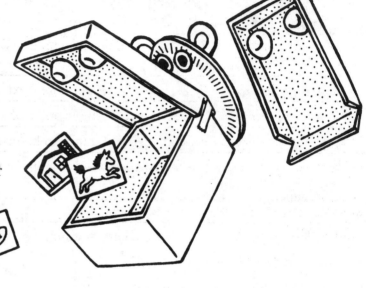

Art Project Instructions

1. Paint the paper plate and the shoe box gray and allow time to dry.

2. Cut two corners of the short end of the lid. Glue two white egg-cup teeth inside the other end of the lid.

3. Tape the lid hinge to the box.

4. Glue a plate to the end of the box and hinge. Place the plate high enough so the box can sit on the table.

5. Decorate the face with large black and white paper eyes glued above the box nose. Paste two small black teardrops at the top of the nose for the hippo nostrils.

6. Cut out two ears from the gray construction paper and glue them to the top back of the uncut plate.

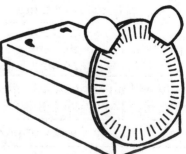

Early Childhood Literacy Checklist

Use this checklist at the beginning, middle, or end of the year to monitor a student's progress in reading, writing, and mathematics.

Child's Name _____ **Date** _____

Student is able to use language to express what he or she sees, hears, feels, and reads.	Yes	No
Student is able to express himself or herself orally and in a written format, such as drawing or printing.	Yes	No
Student shows an interest in exploring rhymes, patterns, and sounds while reading, writing, listening, and using oral expression.	Yes	No
Student participates in discussions about literature, text, and illustrations.	Yes	No
Student is able to listen to others express their point of view.	Yes	No
Student can recognize that oral language can also be printed on paper and read.	Yes	No
Student understands that print is put together to convey meaning, and makes an attempt to understand.	Yes	No
Student makes an attempt to read independently.	Yes	No

Student shows an understanding of book reading:
 	
   a) holds book right-side up
 	
   b) turns pages from right to left
	Yes	No

Student is aware of other cultures, experiences, and lifestyles as represented in literature.	Yes	No
Student shows an understanding of numbers.	Yes	No
Student can demonstrate a one-to-one correspondence between elements in collections.	Yes	No
Student uses manipulatives to count, order, and group.	Yes	No
Student is able to compare and sort objects by their physical attributes.	Yes	No
Student is able to compare and order objects according to attributes.	Yes	No
Student recognizes relationships between concrete representations, number names, and representations of numbers.	Yes	No
Student is able to collect, organize, and describe simple data.	Yes	No
Student can use concrete objects to create, describe, and extend patterns.	Yes	No
Student can recognize geometry in his or her surroundings.	Yes	No
Student recognizes that a single object has different attributes (for example, texture, size, color, length).	Yes	No
Student can use a variety of puzzles and games involving counting problems.	Yes	No

Literacy Awards

I am a doggone great reader!

Beary good reading today!

Beary good reading today!

Beary good reading today!

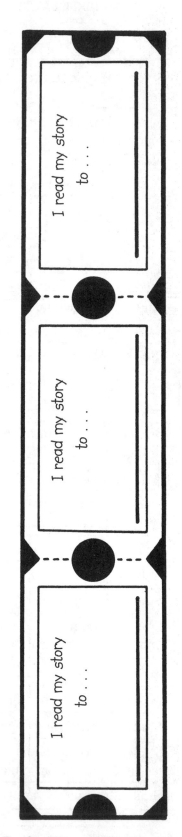

I read my story to . . . .

I read my story to . . . .

I read my story to . . . .

Reading Record Sheet For Students

Name _____

Circle one:						
	☹ 🙂	☹ 🙂	☹ 🙂	☹ 🙂	☹ 🙂	☹ 🙂
Date						
Author						
Book Read						

#3377 Building Literacy Skills Through Art

tall potato chip
container

9" tall (23 cm)

oatmeal
container

7" tall (18 cm)

peanut butter
jar

6" tall (15 cm)

ice-cream
pail

5 qt. (4.75 L)

small plastic
ketchup container

14 oz. (397 g)

small powdered-
drink container

1.9 oz. (53 g)

small Styrofoam
takeout container

5" x 5" (13 x 13 cm)

small, round
nuts container

12 oz. (340 g)

round, plastic individual
pasta container

6" diameter (15 cm)

small plastic
fruit basket

3" x 3" (8 x 8 cm)

small plastic
condiment container

2" diameter (5 cm)

small pudding
cup

2.25" tall (5.6 cm)

tissue box	cube-shaped tissue box	small pudding box
9.25" x 3.5" (23.6 x 9.3 cm)	4.5" x 5" (11.3 x 13 cm)	3.5" x 3" (9.3 x 8 cm)
small cereal box	cracker box	small toothpaste box
11.25" tall (25.6 cm)	10" x 4.25" (25 x 10.6 cm)	1.75" x 5" (4.5 x 13 cm)
mini candy box	small Styrofoam cup	individual-sized milk carton
1.75" x 1.25" (4.4 x 3.1 cm)	8.5 oz. (255 mL)	half-pint (236 mL)
small milk carton	medium-sized milk carton	large milk carton
pint (473 mL)	quart (946 mL)	2 qt. (1.89 L)

Materials Glossary (cont.)

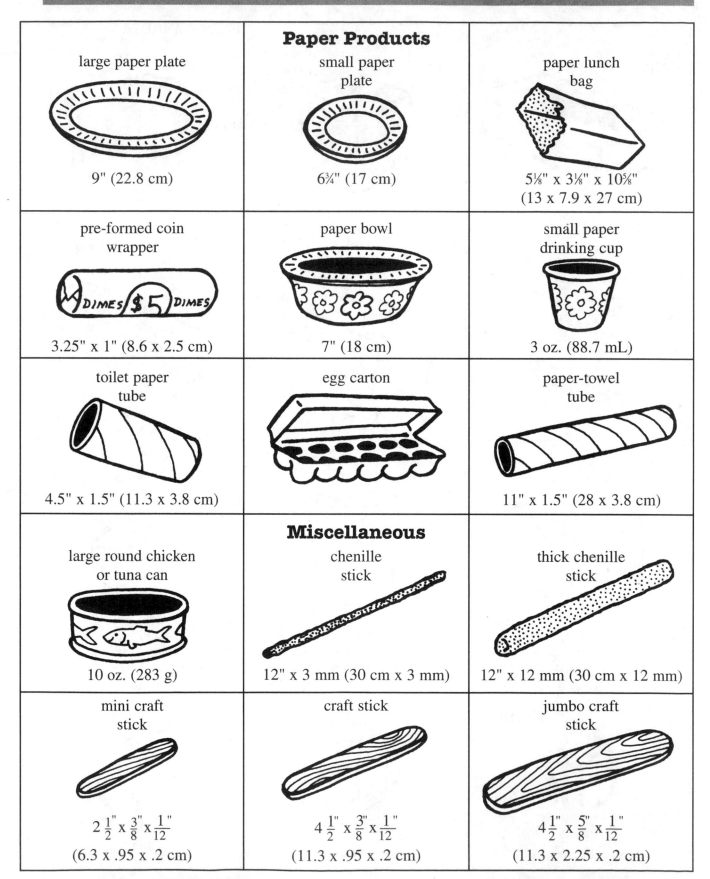

Paper Products

large paper plate
9" (22.8 cm)

small paper plate
6¾" (17 cm)

paper lunch bag
5⅛" x 3⅛" x 10⅝"
(13 x 7.9 x 27 cm)

pre-formed coin wrapper
DIMES $5 DIMES
3.25" x 1" (8.6 x 2.5 cm)

paper bowl
7" (18 cm)

small paper drinking cup
3 oz. (88.7 mL)

toilet paper tube
4.5" x 1.5" (11.3 x 3.8 cm)

egg carton

paper-towel tube
11" x 1.5" (28 x 3.8 cm)

Miscellaneous

large round chicken or tuna can
10 oz. (283 g)

chenille stick
12" x 3 mm (30 cm x 3 mm)

thick chenille stick
12" x 12 mm (30 cm x 12 mm)

mini craft stick
$2 \frac{1}{2}$" x $\frac{3}{8}$" x $\frac{1}{12}$"
(6.3 x .95 x .2 cm)

craft stick
$4 \frac{1}{2}$" x $\frac{3}{8}$" x $\frac{1}{12}$"
(11.3 x .95 x .2 cm)

jumbo craft stick
$4 \frac{1}{2}$" x $\frac{5}{8}$" x $\frac{1}{12}$"
(11.3 x 2.25 x .2 cm)

Materials Index

Tubes

Paper Bowls

Paper Lunch Bag

Cans

Paper Plates

Cups

Egg Cartons

Materials Index (cont.)